Find Your Genius Zone & Differentiate Your Business!

For Business Owners Who Want To Differentiate Themselves And Their Business—So They Don't Have To "Chase" To Get New Clients

Find Your Genius Zone & Differentiate Your Business!

10 Myths Every Business Owner Needs To Avoid To Grow Their Business And Become A Category-Of-One

ROBERTA RAVELLA

The Entrepreneur's Mentor For Business Differentiation

Copyright © Roberta Ravella 2020

All rights reserved. No part of this publication may be reproduced, stored in a retrieval system or transmitted in any form or by any means – electronic, mechanical, photocopying, recording or otherwise – without prior written permission from the publisher.

Published By: Roberta Ravella
Website: www.RobertaRavella.com

PRAISE FOR THE AUTHOR

"I'm a nonbeliever in just about everything, you've got to prove it to me before I will say anything. Well, the coaching I have received from Ravella Coaching Group is top-notch!

I have had Roberta as a coach for two months now and have hired two more people, added a lot more product and actually have a bit of cash flow so I can breathe a little bit. Plus, I am able to get out of the office more to meet people and help them change lives too!

If I could give 10 stars, I would!"

Vikki L.

"Roberta is AMAZING! I had never thought of using a sales coach. I just figured the more people I met, the more likely I would be to get a sale. Silly me!

Roberta teaches you how best to use your time to turn a single sale into a longtime client. She is motivational without being condescending. I would highly recommend contacting her and setting up an appointment."

Chris M.

"After a couple of sessions with Roberta, she helped me to identify who my ideal client was. Once I knew what my ideal client looked like, I could concentrate on marketing to that type of buyer/seller.

Working with my ideal clients has helped my income to increase while my transactions decrease, leaving me to have more personal time with friends and family! It's a good life, and thanks to Roberta, I no longer feel like I have to work 24/7."

Razelle S.

"Roberta is the consummate sales professional. She has excellent people skills and is awesome at maximizing your strengths and minimizing your weaknesses. She constantly inspires you to achieve more and insists on developing your skills as an executive/owner. Working with Roberta has been fantastic."

Daphne J.

"Most leadership coaches only talk about how to lead those in your charge. Roberta reminds us first to lead ourselves and refine our own actions. This is more than leading by example.

Whether you're a Fortune 500 CEO or solopreneur, there's something in Roberta's system for you. The principles she teaches will make you a better businessperson and a better person."

F. Smith

CONTENTS

Introduction 11

Chapter 1   "I Have A Great Offering And I Can Help People, But I'm Often Seen As One Of Many Options" 23

Chapter 2   "Everybody Could Be A Potential Client Because Isn't Sales Supposed To Be A Numbers Game?" 35

Chapter 3   "If I Can Just Work Harder Than Everyone Else, Then I Know I'll Be Successful" 45

Chapter 4   "If I Just Follow A Prescribed Set Of Rules, Do These 10 Steps, Check The Boxes, Buy The System, I'm Guaranteed To Be A Success" 55

Chapter 5   "I'm Told If I Just Follow Passion, I Will Find Happiness And Financial Success" 65

Chapter 6	"I'm Told That The More Value I Deliver Pre-Sale, The More Likely I Will Win The Sale" 75
Chapter 7	"My Business Needs To Be Everywhere In Order To Get Noticed" 83
Chapter 8	"I Need To Be Price Competitive To Win The Sale" 93
Chapter 9	"I Have To Play The Sales Game And Use Typical Sales Techniques" 103
Chapter 10	"I Can Solve My Own Business Challenges. I Don't Need Any Help" 113

INTRODUCTION

If you are reading this book, it's probably because like many business owners, you are starting to feel the pressure of commoditization in your marketplace.

You've noticed more competitors than ever before are influencing your pricing decisions. You feel surrounded, as the competition affects other important choices you make. This could be interfering with important decisions and holding your business back from growth.

When you're swimming in a sea-of-many, how do you differentiate yourself and your business so you can become a category-of-one?

How do you begin to shift your mindset to one where your actions and thinking are completely different than your competition?

These are critical questions you'll be challenged to answer on inside this book. If you want to grow your business and achieve your financial goals, while enjoying your life in the present, it's time to think about differentiating.

Enough Is Enough

Before I became the Entrepreneur's Mentor, I worked in mortgage loan sales for over 20 years. I was taught to just get out there, close the business, and then count my paycheck. My sales manager would actually say to me, "I know it sucks. Count your commission."

Inevitably, I reached the point where they couldn't pay me enough. Before reaching that point, I connected with a coaching group that gave me hope there could be another way to go about this . . . a way that would have me love my life and my business again.

Through them I learned about the 80/20 rule, where 80% of our results come from 20% of our efforts, and how to apply it. I also learned how to discover and work in my unique strengths. Most of all, I found hope that the people I most enjoyed working with were out there—as was the path to help me attract them and stop chasing.

After years of just "sucking it up" and working with any business partner that came my way, what I was learning left me feeling like a light had been turned on. I'm not kidding when I say that the first time my coach told me to fire a realtor, I cried happy tears. That particular business partner had sent me business that made me a lot of money, but he and his clients had been terrible to work with.

My coach reinforced how I was feeling. I couldn't do it anymore. But at the time, I didn't know saying that out loud was even an option. From there, I began changing how I marketed my services, to attract people who were aligned with my own values. Once I started attracting business partners that valued the same things I did, I saw their

INTRODUCTION

customers also valued these things. Soon I ended up with a database of people with similar values.

Business became much better for me. Now, as a mentor and consultant, I help my clients work with these same principles to start attracting the right customer for them.

Get Out Of The Sea

The revelation of differentiating myself from my competition, fundamentally changed the way I do business. Differentiation is especially crucial for people who are in what I call "me-too" industries.

Walk into most networking groups and you will find someone in mortgage, insurance, real estate, financial planning, and so on. These are the people with businesses that fall squarely in the "sea-of-many": businesses that run a typical way, in a typical market. When you're in the sea-of-many, it can seem as though there is no way for you to become a category-of-one, where the seas are calm and there is no competition.

But you can. And if you're serious about your success, you must.

If you're a sea-of-many business, you fight for your piece of the pie. You've probably been taught to work your circle of influence and compete directly against anyone who's in your space. When we don't differentiate ourselves, the market will do so by price. If you're competing on price, you're headed in the wrong direction, quickly. As your competitors continue to lower their prices, how much lower can you go to stay in the game?

If this sounds familiar, it's likely you've failed to figure out who your ideal client is, particularly who your high-value lifetime client is. You've probably not yet identified your unique selling proposition (USP), the key to differentiating your business in a crowded space.

By not knowing your USP, you've neglected to take into account who you are as a person. Do you know what your strengths are? Are you spending 80% of your time doing the 20% of activities you're really good at and enjoy doing?

Without differentiation, you miss out on becoming a category-of-one. You become just another realtor, just another financial planner, just another insurance agency. You're still floundering in the sea-of-many, completely missing the inlet that could lead you to becoming a category-of-one.

Are You Hustling For Value?

If you fail to stand out in a crowded space, and don't become a category-of-one, you will face a shrinking market share. It's just a matter of when, not if, large competitors will try to take over and commoditize what you do. You probably feel that pressure now.

Not only do you have the competition of the others in your space and the frustrated feelings of earning new business

INTRODUCTION

every day, you are also fighting to keep the clients you have. You're hustling for value, but you hate price-competing. Are you tired of hearing "Can I get a better price on that?" Or, worse, "Your competitor will do what you do for less money and work harder."

If you are hearing these phrases regularly, you are being commoditized in the marketplace. You know you're valuable and your business is necessary. So what's really going on?

As a consultant, I work with entrepreneurs across all industries, and I've observed that some industries are simply stuck in old ways. I've seen business owners feeling technology is being pressed upon them, tricked into believing it will differentiate them when it's not the answer.

Anyone can Google anything nowadays. Educating your customers as a way of differentiating yourself just isn't working pre-sale anymore, even if it still works during the transaction. When a customer receives information from you, what's stopping them from taking the valuable information you gave them and going to a cheaper competitor?

If you're resonating with this, you're probably tired of having to do things you don't want to do in order to keep your business going. You feel the pressure to work longer hours, always be available, cold-call customers or continuously participate on social media.

Maybe you just don't fully understand, or are frustrated with, digital marketing. How much money have you spent on gurus, systems, agencies, coaches that promised you results that you didn't get? All the emails and ads sent to you, selling you "proven systems" are, at the end of the day, just empty promises.

Let's be real: You're too smart to follow any box-checking, cheat-sheet type of advice. You're done with tired sales clichés, like, "Sales is a numbers game!" Or worse, "Work harder than anyone!" "Eat frogs first!" "If you were passionate about it, you wouldn't care that it sucks!"

Even worse, you may have been duped into thinking you are either a winner or loser. What if there were no winners or losers? How would this simple change in your thinking affect how you do business?

The fundamental problem is that you remain subscribed to an old way of thinking that just doesn't work any longer. You want the chance to communicate value to your customers, but you feel like you don't have that platform anymore. It's not the platform that's lacking—it's a shift in the way people want to be communicated with. They want to know if you hear their problem and that you are the one they can trust to solve it.

Many business owners, myself included, have been instructed that our value is only what the marketplace dictates.

When I believed that, I only spoke to what I assumed the market valued. It wasn't long before I was second-guessing myself, telling myself I should be doing whatever the latest, shiny new marketing trend was telling me, instead

INTRODUCTION

of knowing—and thereby, doing—what I was excellent at. When you look to the marketplace to tell you who you should be, you miss connecting with your real customers. You miss doing the work you're meant to do.

Are you worried your market is soon to be taken over, or "Uber-ized?" After all, if houses are going to start selling on Amazon, who needs a realtor? The market feels like it's closing in. It feels like you have to work harder and harder to earn the same amount of money, or worse, less money, because your market is shrinking and shrinking. When something is commoditized, people don't pay the same amount for it as they do when they're paying for expertise.

When your perceived expertise shrinks in the marketplace, your income shrinks along with it.

Choose The Broccoli

I wrote this book because I wish somebody would have helped me differentiate myself or at least told me this was all possible much earlier in my career. It's definitely the path less traveled, but it makes the road much easier. It's playing the long game, to be sure, and it's not cheesecake, it's broccoli. But once I had figured out my strengths and my values, then my message was right on point to target the right people.

When you work in your strengths, the external pressure decreases. No one can replicate who you are as a person.

Even better, you can actually earn great money and enjoy who you're working with. Imagine that!

When your values align with your customer's, everything clicks. Without aligning your values, however, you continue to have price pressure and attract less-than-ideal customers—customers who will violate your boundaries or want things from you that you would never do or are uncomfortable doing.

There is no right or wrong when it comes to values alignment. Different people have different values. If money is what you value, you need to be in business with people who value money as well. Once I learned this, it still took another year or two of discovering what it meant to be aligned with my values and how I could start seeing results as fast as possible.

I knew that out of 100 customers, eight would value-align with me; so how could I get to the eight without ever having to talk to the other 92? Was there a way to do that? Maybe not, but I was determined to get as close as I could.

Down The Rabbit Hole

What led me out of "old school" sales was my work with a coach. My coach asked me, "Why aren't you doing what you want?" *"Do I deserve to do what I want?" I asked myself. "Don't we do what we have to do?"* Digging down to the bottom of it, the truth was, my business had become a

INTRODUCTION

job. Most of the time I was not doing work that utilized my strengths and what I was really good at, much less work I wanted to do, even though it made me money and gave me independence.

I had put so much into this career, and now it felt like a 100% JOB. It was time to discover what I really wanted to do. Still, I felt like I was being a quitter, or ungrateful for all my career had afforded me. So I immersed myself in personal development, learning and coaching.

During this discovery period, an insightful email landed in my inbox with the headline: "What is staring you in the face that you are you pretending not to know?" With no hesitation, I wrote down, "I hate my job."

In my mortgage sales career, my bosses were all about their legacy, being top producer, cashing the big checks. There's nothing wrong with it, but 20 years in, I knew these were not my values. I like making money, but I don't need to beat anybody. I no longer believe in winners and losers.

To me, the only "loser" is someone who's living someone else's life.

Once something moves from subconscious to conscious, it has to be dealt with or it will make you miserable. All the pretending I had been doing around the sales spiel: like believing in winners and losers, forcing people to close, the bravado around "I can close anybody"—all of it had been silently draining my energy.

These may work for some people, but for me, it was soul-sucking to be in that belief system. Moving out of that and realizing I could still sell and could still be an entrepreneur was exactly what I needed to move me forward in my career. It was time for the next chapter.

This sent me tumbling down a rabbit hole, learning about high-value lifetime clients and how to determine my unique selling proposition. I took a ton of classes, talked to people, read books. I was grateful to be in a place where I could spend time digging into what it was I wanted to do.

Now, when clients work with me, I offer no cookie-cutter, box-checking solutions. We go all the way down, as deep as possible, into the root of whatever it is that's holding them back. I want to fix things on a structural, bedrock level.

I love helping my clients along the journey towards discovering their own uniqueness and value in whatever industry they're in and watching them confidently move forward in their business on a whole new track. If you're ready to stop chasing customers and hustling for value, this book is for you.

If this book resonates with you and you are ready to shift your thinking and differentiate your business to become a category-of-one, then visit www.RobertaRavella.com/Consult for your Complimentary Business Growth Strategy Consultation (value $795.00).

To your success,

Roberta Ravella
The Entrepreneur's Mentor For Business Differentiation

CHAPTER 1

"I Have A Great Offering And I Can Help People, But I'm Often Seen As One Of Many Options"

"This is pretty exciting! I think they're going to have to fight over us. It's been awhile since I've been a hot ticket. I bet we get some presents!" I said to my husband.

We were picking a firm to guide us through some big decisions, and we had two firms, let's call them Company A and Company B, vying for our attention. The anticipation grew as we scheduled dates for them to court us.

Said anticipation fizzled quickly. From Company A, we endured boring phone calls discussing projections, percentages and positions in the marketplace. My hopes were high that one of them would ask the right questions of us, so we would all know if they might actually help us with what we actually needed. No such luck.

They asked us if we needed anything explained.

No, we are not stupid.

Did we have questions on the information they sent?

No, we can read.

Did we know all of their licenses, tenures with the firms, and what hobbies we can participate with them in if we sign up?

Yes, we know, and thank you, I don't golf, and neither does my husband.

No one from Company A bothered to ask what our needs were or where we were trying to get to. They certainly didn't ask if we trusted them to help us. Talk about exciting.

Seriously though, if you are having trouble sleeping, call me, we can relive the interviews together. Insomnia cured.

I couldn't help but wonder, why do we regale our potential clients with our process and qualifications before ever finding out if we are a good fit? What if we get hours or days in and find out, this just isn't good for either of us?

It may seem obvious, but it keeps happening. Everywhere you look someone is telling you how great their process is for you, and how qualified they are to help you. But they do this without ever asking the questions: What is it that you need? What can I do for you? And actually letting you answer.

My story isn't over, thankfully. We moved on to Company B. When they called, the first thing they asked was, "Hello Ravella Family, what can we do for you? What are your long-term plans? What are you worried about? And, will it be red or white?"

"I HAVE A GREAT OFFERING AND I CAN HELP PEOPLE..."

A few hours later, the doorbell rang. Company B had dropped off a bottle of wine. Needless to say, our choice between A and B was pretty easy.

Stop Competing On Pedigree And Procedure

Yes, you guessed it. Company B got our business. By speaking to our needs and worries first, they successfully differentiated themselves in a busy industry. And there was the wine.

Most of my clients are in crowded spaces. Unfortunately, when it comes to differentiation, many times they turn to their qualifications, procedures, or price. Unless they're heavily recommended, they end up competing on price.

This happened constantly in mortgage sales. Phone calls from people who were referred to me began with, "What's your rate?" These folks had no idea what made me different; they were just told they needed to call a loan officer and get a pre-approval, so they did.

The trouble is, when a conversation opens this way, it is very difficult to redirect the person back to understanding why they might choose you or why they would even compare services. You're already stuck in a commoditized situation.

By competing on price, qualifications or process, you're constantly hustling for value. Your days are filled with the struggle of demonstrating to potential customers why they should pick you. It's exhausting!

Perhaps you are thinking all you have to do to stand out is work 10 times as hard. But working harder just keeps you treading water as you chase clients. It takes a lot of energy; and if you've been playing this game a while, you're probably feeling completely demoralized.

You want to avoid being seen as one of many. But what keeps you stuck in that sea-of-many I mentioned earlier is that you haven't shown the world who you are. You haven't defined your USP. You haven't defined who your ideal client is. You're just marketing to everyone and seeing what sticks. But really, is this approach working for you?

Competency Isn't Enough

If you are still adrift in the sea-of-many, it's likely you haven't gotten clear on your USP. Are you aware of what makes you unique? Do you know what you have to offer, outside of what is market-defined?

Business competency is not enough; it's expected. Sure, you can bake the pie. Get the mortgage. Write the insurance policy. These are just market competencies. By focusing only on competency in your tasks, you miss paying attention to what makes you uniquely capable of helping specific people with their specific problems.

It is easy for business owners to get caught up in the belief that the market dictates our value. This looks like believing you should have certain competencies and these

"I HAVE A GREAT OFFERING AND I CAN HELP PEOPLE..."

are what you should sell on, as opposed to being yourself and attracting people who have the same values as you and need what you alone are uniquely capable of delivering.

Without taking the time to define what you're uniquely capable of and finding the people who need that, you end up selling to everyone. Selling to everyone places you squarely in the sea-of-many, not the category-of-one where you belong.

I know that you're a diligent business owner. I also know that these concepts of working with your USP and your values, while not necessarily new, aren't always discussed in business or sales seminars. When they are discussed, they're spoken about in a way that suggests the function of your USP is basically doing your job right. But doing the job right will not let you stand out in a world where competency is no longer rewarded—it's assumed.

Consider how you do business in your own life. What sets the people you buy from apart?

Imagine you need some landscaping done. You might choose the landscaping company a friend recommends, known for quick, reasonably priced work.

The crew comes to see your yard, but they don't ask you any questions. You feel compelled to ask them about their previous projects. You're moved to base your choice on price and perceived competency.

What if another friend recommends a different landscaping company? They come over, look around your yard, ask a few good questions, and then take your preferences into account. They recognize the problems in your yard, the things that you are concerned about, and once you have asked them if they can help, they draw up a plan just for you.

You forget to ask for previous customer names and exact pricing. You trust them to solve your problem because they earned it by listening to your problems.

We've been taught that our value is market-driven. You bring to the market what it will buy from you, which is usually what you know or are competent at, not what you uniquely have to offer.

Of course, there are some entrepreneurs who are perfectly capable of seeing what industry is hot at the moment and opening up a business in that space. They have a knack for building any business, and that is their unique selling proposition.

When you look at the unique selling proposition of any business, competency is usually assumed. But if you consider other entrepreneurs, like the Richard Bransons of the world, you see that their values and personalities permeate their businesses. There's a reason why they stand out in their industries.

"I HAVE A GREAT OFFERING AND I CAN HELP PEOPLE..."

A New Approach

Coming up in mortgage like I did, I was taught to put on the suit, put on the act, and become a mortgage banker. I was definitely not taught to be myself (I am certain I'm not alone here.)

I recently found myself on the website of a former sales manager. Perusing the staff page, where he and his 10 loan officers were listed, I realized I couldn't tell them apart! Same suit. Same haircut. Same gender. I had to dig into their bios before I could start to distinguish who they really were. Otherwise, they were completely generic.

This uniform approach has been entrenched in business for decades. We're not taught to approach business in a way that speaks to our uniqueness, our values, what we have to offer beyond our competency.

For some people, it might seem a bit "woo-woo" to approach our work this way. Most of the USP classes I've taken were still heavily market-driven. Obviously, you don't want to try and sell something the market doesn't want. But if you're serious about standing out from the rest, you need to be willing to try a new approach.

My own enthusiasm wasn't too high when I decided to go down this road. What led me to this approach was a USP course I took with Perry Marshall. You would have thought I was trying to learn how to perform brain surgery!

FIND YOUR GENIUS ZONE & DIFFERENTIATE YOUR BUSINESS!

That was how resistant I was to looking deeply and determining my best skills. The course involved asking 10 people who knew me really well what they thought my best skill is. The consensus came back as listening. I remember thinking, "Oh, great. How girly."

Having said that, what do we complain about all the time? Surely, you've thought to yourself at one time or another, "That salesperson didn't listen to a word I said!" Listening is a vital quality of a great salesperson. Sometimes we don't value our own strengths.

That was the case with me. In being unwilling to approach this vulnerable edge, you miss discovering and fully valuing what you uncover when you dive in.

You're Not Just An Extension Of Google

When you're seen as one of many options, you never get the respect that you're looking for and deserve. People don't see you as having expertise, they see you as an extension of Google. They just want you to give them information, then they'll make up their minds, and after that, anybody can do the work. They may pick you, but what's stopping them from picking the company that does what you do cheaper or has fancier tech?

This leads to feelings of frustration as a business owner. When you're not able to communicate your value, it's

"I HAVE A GREAT OFFERING AND I CAN HELP PEOPLE..."

painful. When you're not given time to communicate your expertise, you feel misunderstood.

When you do communicate it and you sound no different from the other 10 people with the same expertise, you're just wasting your time. You're constantly chasing clients because they haven't been convinced that you're the right person to solve their problem.

Being seen as one of many options not only causes you to work harder to attract clients, it puts you at risk of not attracting your ideal client. You're working overtime to make it fit. You're always doing things to stand out, like offering price reductions or promises of 24-hour access or solving any and all problems.

From a financial standpoint, when you are seen as one of many, it affects how much you have to spend in advertising, how much time you spend landing those clients you are chasing so hard and your sales conversion rates.

Ultimately, if you remain in the sea-of-many and never become a category-of-one, your business ends up running you. Your ability to set boundaries becomes completely derailed. How long will it take before your business starts feeling like that 9-5 job you used to hate?

The real work of differentiating yourself isn't what you've learned in all the business courses and seminars you've taken. You already have everything you need to start differentiating yourself right now. The question is, are you willing to try a new approach?

Case Study: Mrs. Texas and Mr. MBA

As mentioned, in my previous sales career referral partners, the folks that sent business to me were just as important as the clients themselves. When Mr. MBA reached out to me, I jumped at the chance for a new business partner. The MBA part excited me, as we salespeople are stereotyped as not very smart sometimes. I wanted to work with and be seen as a serious, intelligent businessperson.

We chatted over the phone and scheduled our first mutual client meeting. Mr. MBA set out a few ground rules that he follows for his clients. Certainly understandable. I asked no questions, and just went along for the ride. After all, he was referring clients. I was ready to cash that check.

Did that ever create a recipe for disaster! He called me any day, any time, with demands. Even when I did what he asked, he would have the client call me and ask for more.

Unbeknownst to me, one of his selling points was that he controlled his "vendors." I was selling how hard I work, constant availability and my amazing process instead of selling my niche problem-solving ability. I had to do what he asked because that's what I sold him. It sucked.

The first time I pushed back, he pulled the client from me and gave them to the next person on the list. I had created zero loyalty or differentiation of my services. So the next person in line was just as good. It was a painful but necessary lesson.

Fast forward a few years. We had moved to Texas, and I began the process of building my referral partners. I walk into a real estate office and there sits the most Texas-y person I have ever met. Mrs.

"I HAVE A GREAT OFFERING AND I CAN HELP PEOPLE..."

Texas had high blonde hair and big jewelry and was wearing flashy, sparkling cowboy boots. I thought to myself, this woman will never take me seriously.

She wanted to discuss working together, so I gave it a go.

"This is how I handle my clients and my business," she said at our first meeting. "How do you handle yours?" Wow I thought, no list of demands? "I respect those I partner with. If we are a fit, we should work together." She uttered the magic words . . . *if we are a fit*.

Turns out, her values were the same as mine. She wanted to create a business that she liked and made her good money and wanted me to do the same. We had many pleasant transactions together. We attracted the same type of clients, not demanding and needy, but loyal and fun.

She didn't see me as one of many because I had learned that offering to work all the time and to run my business however was demanded of me actually inspired no loyalty and were not my true unique selling proposition. It's not anyone's.

When your clients and business partners know and match your strengths and your values, a loyal relationship—one where you are seen as the only choice—can be created. Enjoyable work relationships can be created. These things lead to making money AND enjoying your life.

Key Takeaways

- Competency is no longer a differentiator.

- A sharp USP stops price competition.

- When you value-align with your ideal client, they do not see you as one of many.

  "Nobody is superior, nobody is inferior, but nobody's equal either. People are simply unique, incomparable. You are you. I am I."

  - Osho

CHAPTER 2

"Everybody Could Be A Potential Client Because Isn't Sales Supposed To Be A Numbers Game?"

It was happening again. Actually, this time it was even worse. "Hey kid, you don't like steak?" Howie Kendrick, a senior member of the team, ribbed their youngest ball player.

Major league baseball player Juan Soto just took a walk off of six pitches.

"Hey, Juan! You don't like ribeyes?" His teammates teased him. (That's MLB speak for RBI's. Runs batted in=Ribeyes.) Walks don't normally send runners to home plate . . . strikeouts never do.

A few seasons before, Soto's batting had been spotty. He would lose patience and swat at pitches out of the strike zone that he should let go, trying to force a hit. What had changed?

It's a numbers game, right? Swing enough times and you will hit something. Can't get a hit? Your mechanics are off. Still no hits? Time for hours of batting practice.

But then there you are, what seems like a million swings in, it's the bottom of the ninth. A hit wins the game. You have to get that hit. You feel due because after 95 missed swings, surely the universe will smile on you.

As Soto explained, "They told me to look for one pitch in specific, and if it's not that pitch, just don't swing until you have two strikes. I try, and it works. It was easy for me. I just started taking pitches—taking, taking, taking—and then swinging when [the pitcher] is missing [with their intended location]."

So many times in my sales career I found myself swinging. Swinging at whatever—more like whoever—appeared to be the closest sale.

Once the frustration set in, I was going to work and swing and work and swing as hard and as much as I could until something, ANYTHING, stuck. Talk about demoralizing!

It's a numbers game, right? Swing enough times and you will hit something. Pitch enough times and you will sell something. Didn't sell? Your mechanics are off. Can't get a sale? Work more hours!

The mortgage is due. The credit card is past due and top producer bonuses are on the line. Panic sets in. It feels like you will never get out of the dirt. Demoralizing!

Having the patience necessary to stand and wait long enough, to just stop swinging, is the hardest work most of us will ever do.

Sales is so much harder when we do not know who our "right" clients are. When we have the discipline and patience

"EVERYBODY COULD BE A POTENTIAL CLIENT BECAUSE ISN'T SALES..."

to identify them and then wait for it, that's when, just like Soto, we hit the home run.

Stop Swinging At The Wrong Pitches

When I was working in mortgage sales, I cold called a massive number of probable referral partners, attempting to get them to have coffee with me. My hope was that they would find me wonderful at the coffee appointment and would agree to send me business.

This is a pretty common tactic in the mortgage business. Then I started working with a coach, who helped me see what all of us were missing: The coffee appointments weren't bringing in our right referral partners. Or if they were, it was taking a long time to find them. We had to find another way.

I worked on being myself during the calls instead of following canned scripts. Communicating who I was as a person, along with my values, helped attract the right people. Calling my way down the list, I began to see evidence of this approach working. The realtors were either into it or not.

Imagine that! I had to learn to be myself in my business to attract the right people. Before this shift in thinking, I was calling any producing realtor, trying to find a needle in a haystack. It was painful. Finally, I had found a better way.

FIND YOUR GENIUS ZONE & DIFFERENTIATE YOUR BUSINESS!

Put The Phone Down

If you believe in the numbers game, you're probably spending a lot of time pounding. My accountability partner, Judy, calls 100 people every Tuesday. She just goes down a list of names. For her there is zero differentiation in those names.

She's very frustrated. It feels like ditch-digging, and this is coming from a woman who is not afraid to work. She's worried she must be lazy because she hates it so much. But I know that she could save herself the mental and physical agony of it all if she could figure out a way to 80/20 the process. How can she get the people to express their lack of interest in talking to her as soon as possible?

When you believe sales is a numbers game, you risk not just spending hours calling unqualified leads, like Judy does, but also attracting clients who are less than ideal.

One of my clients, Marie, owns a successful diet center. Through her years running the business, she has figured out the precise language that specifically speaks to her high-value lifetime client, which is also connected to her unique selling proposition.

All of her language, everything she talks about in her marketing, her online videos, her questionnaires for potential clients, all of it is geared towards communicating to her ideal client. Despite her efforts, she, too, is susceptible to this myth of "everybody's a potential client."

"EVERYBODY COULD BE A POTENTIAL CLIENT BECAUSE ISN'T SALES..."

Marie's ideal client must be coachable and want to make the changes she will help them with. Knowing this, she still experienced a mismatch with a client. The potential client said, "Sure, I'll do your program, but I can do my own thing too, I don't need you telling me what to do." When Marie replied, "Then I can't take you as a client," the woman blew up. She blamed Marie for not being accommodating, and Marie felt guilty. So she reluctantly took her on.

The woman washed out of the program in three weeks, gave Marie terrible reviews, and continued to speak poorly about her for weeks after!

Now, Marie was somewhat guilted into taking this client. But I hear stories like this all of the time. By believing everyone is a potential customer, you're likely to invite this kind of dynamic into your business.

There's Always Another Customer

Having walked this road before, I can understand if you feel guilty at the thought of being selective. A scarcity mindset kicks in, what if the customer you let go is the last customer you'll ever have?

Then there are the old adages putting pressure on business owners: "Don't leave money on the table!" Expressions like these are reflective of that old-school, churn-and-burn sales mindset, where you just deal with it because it's about the money and therefore about getting enough people on the phone. "Sales is a numbers game" is the oldest sentence in the sales book.

Don't you think it's time to get a new book?

The Future Of Sales

Approaching sales as a numbers game takes a lot of time. You might feel frustrated, constantly selling to people who are not the right fit for you. You feel like you're not working hard enough. But working harder isn't the answer.

Old-school sales rhetoric encourages you to be "tough" and "learn to run to the no." Learn to get over being rejected, because you're going to be rejected all the time. It's true, not everyone is going to buy from you. But if you could set yourself up to be in a place where the majority of people you talk to are at least interested, why wouldn't you?

It's easy to get caught up in the braggadocio: "I made 500 calls today!" or "I talked to 200 people," like it's a virtue. Of course, there is the statistical proof of calling so many people. If you talk to 100 people, you should turn 8% of your calls. But why wouldn't you want to talk to just 50, 20, even 10 qualified leads to get those eight?

While I will discuss this more in Chapter 3, making the calls and getting the numbers carries the same kind of honorable appearance as working hard. It will wear you out though.

"EVERYBODY COULD BE A POTENTIAL CLIENT BECAUSE ISN'T SALES..."

You might think if you had only talked to 500 more people, maybe you'd have gotten 10 more sales. But what if you could have spoken to 50 people who really wanted what you had, made those 10 sales and gone home?

Selling To Everyone Creates Misery

There may be a part of you reading this, thinking, "How can I not take a client? It's money!" But taking on clients that you really don't want is never helpful.

A new business owner contacted me for a coaching consultation. Joseph had an appointment with one of the biggest coaching groups in the area, but he wanted to talk to me first.

"I have to talk to you ASAP!" he said, "The other coach said they would only take my appointment if I had my check book ready."

We spoke about his business, where he wanted to go, what he felt his roadblocks and bottlenecks were. His biggest concern, what kept him up at night, was a fear of making a mistake.

"Roberta, I need to know that I will never make a mistake."

"Joseph," I replied, "Everyone who's anyone in business has made a mistake. Some of them whoppers."

"I am too afraid. If you can guarantee that I won't make any mistakes, I will go with you." His face was intense. I could tell his fears were real.

I also could really use that check. It was early in my coaching career, and business costs were growing at a faster rate than clients. Was being honest a mistake?

"Joseph, I can only guarantee that I will help you make the best decisions possible. And when you fail at something, when the mistake happens, we'll work it out together."

He seemed sad at my answer.

"You should go to your other appointment. I don't think I am the right coach for you."

He did and signed up with the false promise of zero mistakes.

If I had said, "Joseph I will match their no mistakes guarantee," it would have been the first lie in our relationship. "Any client" would have kept me up at night, worrying about inevitable mistakes. I had to let it go.

If you're playing a numbers game and take any client, any customer, anyone who sends you business, you're making life way harder than it needs to be. When we sell to everyone, it creates misery.

"EVERYBODY COULD BE A POTENTIAL CLIENT BECAUSE ISN'T SALES..."

Case Study: From Half A Day To 90 Minutes

My coaching client, Daniella, bought lead lists from her parent company. The leads had entered their contact information on the corporate website so they could learn more about their benefits. She was calling this huge list and having a really, really hard time with it.

It felt like cold calling. But she was learning how to tell, as early as a few seconds in, whether the person wanted to get off the phone or not.

We redid her script in a way that was designed to help these people open up more. She still hated it and felt lazy for hating it. She had started working as an independent contractor so as not to have to do work she hates. With these calls, Daniella was back in what felt like a 9-5 job, where her boss had given her a list of names to call. But she's the boss!

It brought up a lot of negative feelings, like that persistent feeling of laziness, which was just not true. She's one of the most self-motivated and hardworking people I know.

We decided she should compile her own list. This time with names of people whom she had contact with over the previous couple of years. A warm list.

Over the course of my work with Daniella, I helped her move from working with hundreds of faceless people who at some time said, "Sure, I might want some financial information," (which they can get anywhere) to working with this new list of people who have raised their hands and said, "I want information from you, Daniella."

It's going so much better. She's getting to the, "No, thanks for calling" or the "Yes! I am so glad you called me back" much quicker. She's swinging at pitches she has a good chance of hitting. The closing ratio is WAY up. Time spent, WAY down. No more feeling lazy or inadequate.

As Daniella's story shows, working in our strengths and as closely as possible to attract our ideal customers brings us to the results we were looking for much faster and with much less frustration.

Key Takeaways

- "Everyone" is not your customer.

- Design your sales model so it gets you to your high-value customer as soon as possible.

- Knowing your USP and your values will keep you out of the numbers game.

    "Insight and doing what we ourselves want leads to high returns."

    - Richard Koch

CHAPTER 3

"If I Can Just Work Harder Than Everyone Else, Then I Know I'll Be Successful"

There it was again . . . another call schedule with scripting and a spreadsheet for daily tracking.

With advice from a tenured, successful business coach, I was going to dive back into cold calling. Not my favorite thing. But I have done it before. And no pain, no gain.

Like most coaches, my first year had been tough. If I wanted to make it go, I was going to have to put in some serious work. Nothing seems like more serious work than 800 cold calls.

I couldn't wait to tell my accountability partner that I had struggled through. Done the deed. Worked oh so hard!

Until I reviewed the results sheet. This lady had made 800 calls in a month to qualified prospects. Her sales skills are top notch, yet the result after multiple appointments was ONE prospective client.

Most people would say, "Wow, she worked really hard!" And she did. But to what end? Needless to say, I did not make those calls.

FIND YOUR GENIUS ZONE & DIFFERENTIATE YOUR BUSINESS!

The lever applied, in this case, hard work, was getting this coach nowhere.

We have been taught that hard work cures all ills. We have been taught that hard work is the only way to get ahead. But what if you could find the easiest path, with integrity of course, to get the result that you want in the least amount of time?

Where would you start? The 80/20 Principle.

Apply The Right Lever

We know that 80% of our results are caused by 20% of our efforts. Sometimes it's 90-10 or even 95-5.

Obviously, we need to work at what we want to obtain; nothing worthwhile comes free. You have to work harder than most other people to be successful. But working just to work? It is not a virtue. Like Michael Jordan once said, "I'm not out there sweating just to feel myself sweat."

The concept of hard work being a virtue is deeply entrenched in business and society. We have "no pain no gain" drilled into our heads. That 95% of the journey will be horrible, so hard, you are going to HATE it! You must knuckle down, and pay your dues!

It's a belief that's passed along through the decades. But the truth is, working harder than anyone else does not guarantee success.

"IF I CAN JUST WORK HARDER THAN EVERYONE ELSE..."

Don't believe me? Look around. There are plenty of people working their butts off. Ask the landscapers in your front yard if they're working hard. They are working hard! Unless they own the company, they're not getting ahead. They're just paying their bills.

Entrepreneurship today is no longer about working harder, hardest; it's about applying the right lever to the right place.

It's for those who know constant force applied over time in the right direction will get them the farthest toward where they want to go—and they won't be burned out when they get there.

What good is all that money if you are so stressed out, your relationships are ruined and you are too physically run down to enjoy it?

Stop The Spinning

I've seen so many business owners working really hard yet feeling like they're just not getting ahead. Buying into the "work your butt off" myth means that, more often than not, you end up spinning your wheels.

Believing in working harder has been exacerbated in today's world where we're connected all the time. Now you probably think you have to work around the clock, just because you can. People seem to expect it.

Constant connection as a means of working harder brings its own set of problems. I consulted with two women who owned an eldercare business. They have an amazing business. During our meetings, they would put their phones away. But one of them, despite putting her phone down, would still receive notifications on her Apple watch. She could barely garner any good from our time, as the watch demanded her attention.

Here's the thing: these women were stressed out! They were working 15-hour days and then going home to do more paperwork. Being connected 24/7 didn't help. Buying into the myth of working harder had them living on a vicious treadmill.

Incessant hard work is not sustainable. What's falling by the wayside because you're working so hard? Many business owners I've worked with needed convincing to hire outside help, whether to fulfill a role in the business or just take care of their homes. Women, especially, feel guilty about outsourcing housework even though they are running themselves ragged.

The myth of hard work easily leads to believing we should do it all. But even if we could do it all, do we really want to?

Certainly, there are times we do have to work hard. But when you start seeing diminishing returns, despite pulling 60-hour weeks, or you're no longer effective, mental and physical burnout is fast approaching.

"IF I CAN JUST WORK HARDER THAN EVERYONE ELSE..."

Get To Know Your True Value

The value Western business culture places on productivity is hard to get away from. Yet adhering to it mires you in the myth of working harder. After all, busy equals important.

Think of the interactions you have with people—how long does it take them to ask you what you do for work when you first meet? This is where we place our value. Even looking at the court system, if you are sued or sue someone, the court wants to know how much you earn—they need to ascertain how much you're worth, and what you're worth is what you earn or produce. How we value people in our court system is a good indicator of where a society places value.

Consider your own beliefs here: I know it's easy to believe that the harder someone works, the more valuable or important they must be, right? How many times do you ask people how their business is doing? Or how busy they are? People ask me all the time, "Are you busy?" Just because I'm busy doesn't mean that my business is good! Early in my career, I felt important when I was busy. Then I finally clued into the fact that it was ridiculous.

Because we place so much value on "busy", if we're not persistently productive, it feels like we're not working hard enough. It's unfortunate we don't consider time alone, time for creativity, time with friends and family, or time for our spiritual endeavors as productive. Culturally, we have this need to feel like we worked.

FIND YOUR GENIUS ZONE & DIFFERENTIATE YOUR BUSINESS!

People shame others for not working hard enough. I know I've experienced it. I've had business partners blatantly appalled at the idea I might take a vacation and they won't be able to reach me. And I gave in to it.

On vacation in Italy, I took phone calls while my husband was eating gelato in a beautiful seaside café. For what? So I could say I was "the hardest worker"? There I was, in a beautiful town on the Mediterranean, on an amazing vacation... and I'm working?

The "work hard enough and you'll succeed" mindset permeates our culture. It's the meta-narrative of the American Dream. If we just work hard enough, we can be/do/have whatever we want.

The puritanical work ethic was entrenched further by a system that wanted to build and maintain a healthy workforce of worker bees. But that system is broken.

The worker bees who exist now in the US struggle to feed their families. You can no longer get a factory job that will last 30 years and give you a good pension for your hard work. Much less put kids through college or take a decent vacation.

As a result the younger generation has increased their entrepreneurship. They've watched their parents commute a distance, work all day, come home at seven or eight at night, then get a 3% raise every year. And they are working hard!

"IF I CAN JUST WORK HARDER THAN EVERYONE ELSE..."

Many educators in the US talk about changing the education system from producing worker bees to training critical thinkers. This is an example of changing the lever.

Moving from teaching people to reproduce a task over and over, to developing their critical thinking skills, becomes a necessity as we head deeper into a world dominated by technology and artificial intelligence.

Seen in this light, the question becomes: would you rather be a worker bee, working in your business, or a critical thinker, working on your business?

There's A Pill For That

A company that I worked for actually encouraged us to work holidays and weekends (unless you hated money, of course, then you didn't have to.) Needless to say, I had my first panic attack there. I went to the owner of the company requesting to slow down a bit because it was overwhelming. His suggestion? "Go to my doctor and get some pills. Everybody here is on pills." And it was true! Nearly everyone there was on Xanax, Prozac or some other equivalent.

There was no way I was going to sacrifice my health for money. It was obvious to me then, and remains now, that working harder and harder in hopes of achieving success creates a level of stress which will exhaust your body, and your mind.

Working hard for the sake of working hard will leave you feeling overwhelmed and, worse, trapped. When I was working so hard, I felt trapped. All of the hard work felt useless. It was never enough.

Consider how much it's worth to you, all the hard work you're doing. Is it worth straining important relationships? Is it worth missing holidays? Are you working so hard for something you will never have the time to enjoy? What is all this hard work really for?

Case Study: Debbie Stops Chasing

Debbie, a real estate agent and client of mine, had a robust database of people who had used her services before. She was also on a team that gave her leads from the internet, leads they had paid for.

The idea was to build the paid leads into an additional referral base, boosting Debbie's sales and income.

It was incredibly hard work. She had to chase these people down around the clock. Out of 100 people, she would close four or five. The process was time-consuming, and although some of them referred again, the majority didn't.

When Debbie came off the team, I went through her entire database and together we hammered out who her top referring customers were. Armed with this knowledge, she marketed heavily to only those customers. By taking the 80/20 approach to her database,

"IF I CAN JUST WORK HARDER THAN EVERYONE ELSE..."

within six months Debbie made more money than she had the entire year before.

The next year she reached her new annual income goal in August. We focused on repeat business which raised her average sales price, therefore raising her average commissions. The best part? With the increase, she hit the income goal with fewer transactions than the entire year before.

Weekends are now by appointment only. Otherwise she and her 100% debt-free family will be swimming in their new pool.

Stories like Debbie's abound in the business space, yet I see so many business owners stuck on "if I can just work harder." Give yourself a break. If you're reading this, you work hard already. Wouldn't it be nice to work less and profit more, like Debbie did, without all the blood, sweat, and tears? If you found yourself nodding yes, the good news is, it is quite possible.

Key Takeaways

- Our value is not defined by what we produce.

- Working hard for the sake of working hard leads to diminishing returns and deteriorating relationships.

- There are three common levers: work, time, money. Use the 80/20 principle to apply the work lever to its most valuable place.

FIND YOUR GENIUS ZONE & DIFFERENTIATE YOUR BUSINESS!

"A starving heart or mind cannot produce its best work. Never feel guilty for nourishing yourself."

- Megan Macedo

CHAPTER 4

"If I Just Follow A Prescribed Set Of Rules, Do These 10 Steps, Check The Boxes, Buy The System, I'm Guaranteed To Be A Success"

If you've ever been on a diet, you know most weight-loss programs count on their customers following their programs or systems for success. But as any dieter also knows, and I say from personal experience, these programs and systems don't always work.

Rules, steps, boxes or systems are never a guarantee of success. If they were, we'd see way less people moving onto the next diet after regaining any weight they lost while using someone's "proven system."

In my experience, the "proven" diet program I bought was not what led me to sustainable weight loss. Five years ago, I used one such system. It seemed to work at the time, but any results I got didn't last for long. It wasn't until I changed my thinking that I actually achieved sustainable weight. I had to do things that were outside of the system I bought in order to have long-term success.

It's not just the diet industry that tells us to buy the proven system. As a coach I was told to buy a system or buy a franchise (I'm glad I didn't!). I'm sure whatever space you're in, you have been told that if you buy the system and check the boxes, your success is guaranteed.

Many a guru says, "My way is the only way for you to get where you want to go." When you hear that, get the check book out, they're about to sell you something.

When we go for a "proven system," we rarely question what principles are being applied. We are in it for the quick fix.

Technique is technique; we can learn technique over time. Put anything into a system and it will run, but this is not necessarily success. By thinking this way, we're not pushing ourselves to think on the level of principles.

Banking our success on a plug-and-play system means we ignore the principles that really drive success—principles like self-awareness, integrity, 80/20, or simplification.

Plug And Play Doesn't Pay

The harsh truth is, running your business using someone else's "proven" system is inauthentic. Doing so demonstrates neglected values, both yours and your customers'. If you're just plugging in a system and the person who created the system doesn't have the same values as you, even though you might have some success at the start, eventually it will stop working for you.

IF I JUST FOLLOW A PRESCRIBED SET OF RULES, DO THESE 10 STEPS..."

Worse, when you're plugged into a system that opposes your values, you're not showing up as yourself. Eventually it wears you down. Having to pretend to like things or people you don't really like, and saying yes to things you don't want, can lead to feelings of anger and resentment, and eventually burn out.

These feelings become underlying forces in your psyche. Now you feel bad about what you are doing in your work, and soon enough, you're out there hustling for value. Wouldn't it be easier just to be yourself?

I've seen many people in the mortgage business live out this myth. The gurus would say: "Do exactly what I'm doing, say exactly what I'm saying." People taking this advice lost the integrity of their authentic voice. There was no room for their values to be known. There was certainly no avenue for attracting ideal clients through value alignment.

I've also seen business owners become disappointed with the systems and programs they bought. You paid the money, bought the system, and now you don't like the fit and have to struggle through it. Sometimes you feel like you have to force yourself to follow through. This is a good indicator the system is neither working to your strengths nor connecting with your values.

FIND YOUR GENIUS ZONE & DIFFERENTIATE YOUR BUSINESS!

To Reinvent Or Not To Reinvent

If you've bought into this myth, it's likely because on some level, it is smart. We've been counseled time and again not to reinvent the wheel. It's common practice for people who want to be successful: Find somebody who's already done it, see what they did, and copy them.

I don't disagree with this, but we need to push ourselves to think and act on a higher level.

Buying into this myth keeps us looking for technique, not cause and effect, when there may be a million techniques to produce the results we're seeking.

Since we started with diet, let's consider exercising. We know cardio workouts help people lose weight. There are a gazillion ways to get a cardio workout in. Still, when I see my friend lose 50 pounds by running, I'm tempted to try it.

The trouble is, I detest running. Now I'm telling myself I have to run to lose weight. But because I hate it and I'm not good at it, I'm going to struggle plugging into that system.

Meanwhile, there are so many other ways to get my heart rate up. Why wouldn't I just try one that I like? One that I can do long-term?

For me that activity is indoor cycling, otherwise known as spinning. I'm in a cold dark room. Dance music is blaring, the occasional disco lights flash, and some crazy instructor is yelling out instructions from the front of the room. By the end of class I am sweat-soaked, exhausted and satisfied. I

IF I JUST FOLLOW A PRESCRIBED SET OF RULES, DO THESE 10 STEPS..."

bet all of you runners out there just thought YUCK! But this is a workout I can happily do several times a week.

When consistency is required, sustainability becomes a must.

Focusing on technique limits your thinking, leaving you unable to see the multiple methods to producing the same results you think you will get from one program. By only allowing for one path, you're stuck in a dark, narrow tunnel where all you can see is the light of the plug and play and nothing else.

Expand your thinking to a place beyond techniques to higher principles of cause and effect. Then you can find a process or system that fits with your values and strengths, leading to sustainability.

A wise diet guru once said, and I paraphrase, we want a pill to sustain our unhealthy life, instead of doing the real hard work of changing our mindset around food and exercise. The same with business owners who want a prescription for success. It's scarier to do the inner work of growing self-awareness and figuring out one's strengths and values. You may worry about what you'll find when you open the Pandora's box that is your innermost self.

This opening up can send you into a spiral of self-doubt: What if I can't reproduce the results? What if I'm not creative enough? What if I'm not smart enough? What if I'm not good enough? So rather than face any feelings of inadequacy

59

that might come up, you click "buy" on that box, system or program.

When you're so hungry for something that works, you'll be tempted to buy the proven system. It's just like the diets. Why does anyone buy Atkins bars or do the cabbage soup diet? Because, at first, it appears to be a system that works (even though it's not the healthiest, and more often than not the weight returns.) But sometimes we feel like we just need something that works.

Are You Ignoring The Real Change?

If you've bought into this myth, you are at risk of compounding the damage by skipping around, starting with one program, then shifting to another, costing time and money. More than likely, you end up returning to how you did things before.

Take a closer look at what keeps you stuck buying programs or bouncing around between systems. Is there a behavior change you know you need to make but are resisting? Buying someone else's system is an easy way to bypass the effort required to apply more effective principles or change your behavior.

Maybe you don't want to change the inconsistency in your sales model. A "proven system" is a surefire way to bypass the effort it will take to change in a meaningful way. This is one reason people buy fad diets. They don't want to

IF I JUST FOLLOW A PRESCRIBED SET OF RULES, DO THESE 10 STEPS..."

change their behavior; they want a fix. The diet helps them bypass what's hard—meaningful change.

This suggests lazy thinking. But you're not lazy, you're just tired of beating your head against a wall!

I get it, choosing the proven system offers relief. When you're plugging away and you just can't get ahead, then you see the promise of a system you can buy off of the shelf; of course you feel a sense of relief.

Just like a crash diet, it works for a while, but before you know it, everything reverts back to the way it was before.

When this happens, what do you do? Go for another system? Doing so ignores the foundation of the problem. Without taking time to push your thinking to a higher level, you'll never get over the hump. How much money do you want to spend on systems that don't work?

Sometimes it's more than pushing yourself to think higher. If you're not feeling confident in doing the work it takes to change, you are more likely to buy the program. I've done it myself. I bought the program and in the middle of it I realized that I hated it and I was avoiding the real work. Talk about flushing money down the drain!

The things we think give us confidence are rarely what actually bring us confidence. By believing in the "proven system" myth, you're choosing someone else's program over listening to your intuition, becoming self-aware and aligned with your own values.

Case Study: There Are Many Ways To Close The Deal

A colleague of mine, Sue, and I used to make cold calls together. Our coaching group had a 12-week protocol for calling prospects that we completed as part of our commitment. Neither Sue nor I wanted to do it, but our coach told us we needed to do it, and that everyone who was successful was doing it. It worked well for the company founders, so why not go for it?

So here Sue and I went, hopping on the phones together. Every Monday for 12 weeks, we made our calls. Did it work? I had some success. But I hated it! I did it anyway, but it was a struggle. I could only do it for so long.

But Sue? It caused her so much stress. She grew to hate the appointments. It didn't help her improve on the phone, and she had trouble with phone calls for a long time afterwards. Sure, it pushed her out of her comfort zone, but she found meeting potential business partners face to face worked much better for her. In those situations, she excelled. The cold calling was of no benefit to Sue at all—other than to connect her with her values and strengths through the contrast.

At the time, both of us needed to meet new referral partners. Although there are many ways to go about it, cold calls were the cheapest and most systematized and could be easily tracked.

However, a better approach would have been for Sue and I to analyze where our strengths were and find a method to fit them (of which there are many). When Sue found the confidence to listen to herself and trust her instincts, she found the technique that produced the

IF I JUST FOLLOW A PRESCRIBED SET OF RULES, DO THESE 10 STEPS..."

best results. Meeting potential business partners fact to face, where they "lived" worked decidedly better for Sue.

In business, you can find systems and programs to help you with almost anything. Wouldn't you rather find that one coach, consultant or mentor who will help you truly change your mindset? Or the program that will deeply change how you think about yourself and your business?

Key Takeaways

- Change your thinking at the highest level to avoid the entrepreneurial rollercoaster.

- Authenticity leads to sustainable success.

- Find patterns in your business that will become your unique systems.

"Your time is limited, so don't waste it living someone else's life. Don't be trapped by dogma—which is living with the results of other people's thinking. Don't let the noise of other's opinions drown out your own inner voice. And most important, have the courage to follow your heart and intuition. They somehow already know what you truly want to become. Everything else is secondary."

- Steve Jobs

CHAPTER 5

"I'm Told If I Just Follow Passion, I Will Find Happiness And Financial Success"

When it comes to passion, some people are really passionate about what they do, and some people aren't. It's that simple. When you believe following passion leads to happiness and financial success, you might be selling yourself short.

I've known the guy who handles my home insurance for a long time. I call him the "insurance nerd" because he's the only person I've ever met who's seriously passionate about insurance. Anything you want to know about any kind of insurance, he'll talk about it until you stop him. He just loves it.

Contrast him with a roofer I know. We've had long talks about business. During one of our talks he said, "Who cares about roofing?" He just wasn't in it for the roofing.

He certainly focused on excellence, had all his licensures, and gave the highest-level guarantee that you can possibly give—that's the kind of person he is. He may have landed in the industry by circumstance, but he's not going to do anything halfway.

Roofing is not an easy job. For starters, it's hot up there! You have to deal with insurance companies, sometimes convince people they need it done, and then you deal with the laborers. Roofers can make a lot of money, but it's hard, hard work. So, I had to know, why was he doing it?

"I can never say no to my wife. The money means I never have to," he grinned. Speaking about his wife, his whole face lit up. If his wife, or anyone in the family, needs something, he hates telling them no.

My insurance agent is passionate about his work. The roofer? Less so. He has the value of and conviction for excellence, but his passion was elsewhere. Did he have financial success and happiness? Sure he did. But these did not come from a passion for roofing.

It's Okay To Be Passion-Free

We can lock ourselves into tunnel vision when it comes to passion. If you buy into this myth and don't actually feel passionate about your work, you could feel like there's something wrong with you. There isn't!

Believing this myth and not connecting to a passion can perpetuate a feeling of inadequacy. You might find yourself jumping around a bit, either in career or in methodology, as you try to determine how to turn your work into something you're passionate about.

"I'M TOLD IF I JUST FOLLOW PASSION, I WILL FIND HAPPINESS..."

You may feel like you're just punching a clock or slogging through. You're trying so hard. But is passion what's really missing?

When I worked in mortgage, there was so much money and opportunity that I tried to convince myself to be passionate about it. I was also pretty darn good at it.

But being passionate about something and being good at it are not the same thing. Later, after I left the business, people told me they could tell how hard I was trying and that it wasn't clicking.

Get Off The Passion Train

When it comes to passion, it doesn't help that a pile of business and self-help gurus harp on this meme. How often do you hear people like Oprah talking about finding your "passion" and never "working" another day in your life? And how disappointed does it make you feel? Or perhaps you feel like you are missing something?

How many times have you heard a story of the person who was stuck in their 9-5 job, then discovered how much they love working with art and kids so they started a business selling art supply subscription boxes and now they're billionaires?

Of course, businesses like these or like Spanx, to use a real-life business, are great examples of people who solved problems they were passionate about. But this isn't for everybody, and it can be damaging to believe it should be.

Author Elizabeth Gilbert learned to reframe how she talks about passion. She had given her "Find Your Passion" talk one day when a woman in the audience confessed to Gilbert how upset it had made her. This woman felt hurt by the talk because she had never found her own passion. Every time she heard Gilbert say, "You have to find a passion," it landed as, "If you haven't found a passion, you can't have a good life."

But this woman did have a good life, and she knew it. She liked the things she did, and she also liked moving on to other things.

Gilbert felt prompted to learn more from this woman, and survey other people. Her research revealed that for some people, passion is the driver. And for others, it isn't. She came up with a metaphor: jackhammers, for those who need to be in love with what they're doing and are singularly focused on it, and hummingbirds, who go from beautiful thing to beautiful thing.

There is nothing wrong with being passionate like Elizabeth Gilbert or my insurance nerd friend. It becomes wrong when you falsely believe you must be passionate, and you just aren't. My roofer friend runs a stellar business even though he could care less about roofing. Of course, he cares about excellence and serving the customer, but a passion for it isn't what fuels the work.

"I'M TOLD IF I JUST FOLLOW PASSION, I WILL FIND HAPPINESS..."

What Lights You Up?

Ultimately, believing in this myth means attaching your happiness to something that may be completely untrue for you. Every individual is unique. What lights you up? Can you dare to find it without tripping on this myth and coming up short?

Passion doesn't apply to all business owners, even though you probably think it does. How often do you worry that you haven't found the thing that makes you want to jump out of bed and run to the office? And then feel bad about yourself after worrying?

At my first mortgage company, the men I worked with were bankers, through and through. They wore three-piece suits. They golfed. And they loved the lives they were building. As owners of the company they valued money, wealth and legacy. For them, those values were their purpose.

They were going to do whatever it took—legally, of course!—to secure their wealth and legacy and they'd do it 1000 times. They were passionate about building wealth and legacy, and they did not need a passion for the work itself.

These guys were from a different generation, one where they were taught that whether they loved or hated their job, the outcome is a great paycheck so stop complaining. But they didn't just take it, they liked it. They were fine with it. Was it a grand passion? No, but all they had to do was look at their paychecks and their values of wealth, family and legacy were met.

By spending too long digging around for a passion that may or may not exist, you're losing precious time connecting to your values. You avoid focusing on what you are trying to build. My mortgage bankers and roofer had found their purpose, their mission, and the work served to fulfill it.

It's Not Worth Feeling Inadequate

When you've been hammered with the message you need passion to succeed, yet you just don't feel it, you feel like you're lacking in some way. Your confidence takes a hit. Worse, you can't differentiate your business.

If that roofer felt he had to be passionate about his business or he was going to lose out, he could have left the roofing business and gone looking for something else. But he didn't because he's able to see that his values are being met. He found his purpose outside of himself and it kept him going when things were hard.

The woman who told Elizabeth Gilbert that her words were hurtful to her felt inadequate. She'd been searching and digging for this thing, thinking "I'm supposed to have this, and I can't find it. What's wrong with me? There must be something wrong with me. Am I a bad person?"

That was how I felt at the mortgage company. I tried so hard to be passionate about the work—when in actuality I

"I'M TOLD IF I JUST FOLLOW PASSION, I WILL FIND HAPPINESS..."

did not like it, especially when I was around other people who were passionate. I felt out of place. Worse, I struggled to land the right clients because I was ignoring my own values.

You bypass the ability to connect with your ideal client if you're living under this myth. It can lead you down the slippery slope of selling to everybody. After all, if you're so passionate about it, everybody should want it. That just never works.

Case Study: Australia or Bust!

This is a story about purpose over passion. A guy in my mortgage coaching group, we'll call him Ben, had built quite a successful business. He ran all of the sales, and his staff did the fulfillment. His purpose in life was to spend as much time as he could with his wife and six kids. They wanted to live comfortably, give heavily to their church and travel the world.

At one of our mastermind sessions he regaled us with a tale of a recent trip to Australia. His staff was prepped and ready to handle everything, so he turned off his phone, jumped on a plane, and took the family halfway around the world for a month.

Transfixed with Ben's story, we fired out questions: How did it go? How many bad problems did you have? Did you lose customers? More important, did you lose MONEY?

We hung on every detail, all so excited he had reached what seemed to be an unattainable goal. The trip had been a family and business success.

FIND YOUR GENIUS ZONE & DIFFERENTIATE YOUR BUSINESS!

A few years later, I ran into his coach at a sales conference. "Hey Iris, how is Ben doing? Where else has he taken the family?" A disappointed look came over her face. What could have happened, I thought.

"Well, he got caught up in a group of mortgage guys that were way into hiring salespeople and building huge offices. He convinced himself that, if he was so passionate about building his mortgage business, he could not stop growing as big and building as much as humanly possible."

Hire mores salespeople! Close more volume! Be more passionate than anyone!

It took less than a year to undo everything he had worked for. Now chained to his "big boss" desk, there was no way he could go on vacation, much less for a month or with no phone. The family was at home waiting for him most nights.

"That's so unfortunate, Iris. Why did he do it? Seemed like he had it all worked out," I said, dejected.

He lost his purpose for someone else's passion. He thought that being passionate about helping others become as successful as he was made him a better person. Nothing wrong with that, of course, but he missed sticking with his purpose when it didn't fit in with what the "big boys" around him were doing.

Being the great coach that she is, Iris had him on a plan to get back on track. He returned his office to the original size and only worked on sales with his staff handling fulfillment systems. The family made it back out to see the world, all while making tons of money again.

"I'M TOLD IF I JUST FOLLOW PASSION, I WILL FIND HAPPINESS..."

Passion can be developed over time and can wane over time. It can lead us astray. It's important to recognize its limits. Finding your purpose and focusing on what you care about aligns what you enjoy doing with your values and the impact that you want to have in the world.

Key Takeaways

- Your passion may be outside your work.

- Values alignment is more important than passion.

- Value self-awareness. Not everyone's rhetoric is yours; discover for yourself what you need.

    "Happiness is not ready made. It comes from your own actions."

    - **Dalai Lama**

CHAPTER 6

"I'm Told That The More Value I Deliver Pre-Sale, The More Likely I Will Win The Sale"

While content marketing is what we use to attract people to our message, one of the most common mistakes I see business owners make is over delivering value pre-sale, thinking it guarantees the sale. When it comes to content, strategy over quantity wins every time.

Many times you get an initial consult request from potential clients, referred or otherwise, and then dive straight into sending the person all kinds of information, telling the client how the process works and offering solutions without having diagnosed the problem. This causes a missed opportunity to show that you understand their problem and to build trust that you are the one to solve it.

You believe that if you give tons of value pre-sale, you're guaranteed a client. But doing this completely misses how we get people to trust us in the first place! If you're too busy telling the prospect everything about your system, are you listening to them?

FIND YOUR GENIUS ZONE & DIFFERENTIATE YOUR BUSINESS!

We think content marketing is about how much information and value we can give away for free. But I've seen often enough how people will take all the information I just gave them and go somewhere cheaper. Or more likely, take the information to someone they really trust.

I had this happen to me in mortgage. I'd solve somebody's loan problem, only to have them take it to the banker they really wanted to use anyway. I never gave the potential client the opportunity to trust me. I blurted out the solution before they had a chance. Before listening to their real problem.

It's rarely the first thing they mention. "My credit may be messed up from losing my job a few years ago" actually means, "I am embarrassed that we can't get the best rate and program because of my job situation."

By shoving education and information at them, I missed out on gaining their trust.

Failure To Connect

In today's business world, we see people giving content before connecting with their prospects. Content marketing seems to be all about a massive delivery of information. To make this marketing model work requires so much more than just dumping out free content about your processes and systems.

If we use our pre-sale time to ask about the prospect's problem and find out what they really need, we can

"I'M TOLD THAT THE MORE VALUE I DELIVER PRE-SALE..."

determine if we are a right fit, if it's a win-win. And the client can decide if they trust us to help them solve their problem.

I see business owners constantly telling their prospective clients they will educate them 100% on everything pre-sale. Why would I join them in doing this? I'm not Google. And searching on Google is all anyone has to do to find out what these people are sharing.

There's a big difference between being an information bank and helping a potential client with their problems. Once they know they can trust us to solve their problem, it's a good time for education and information. Until then your clients are looking for transformation, not information.

You know you're stuck in this myth if you're over-delivering and not being strategic about the value you are sharing through your marketing. Yes, you have to give, but who are you speaking to?

Focusing on yourself—i.e., how much value you're giving pre-sale—can lead to missing your customer's problems entirely. Simply put, educating people is not reaching their pain points. It's never going to differentiate your business.

I get it; it's easier to do this kind of information selling. It's also easier to explain what it is you do, rather than dig into the market research and really figure out where your customers are struggling.

You can show up to your customer's office with whatever your product is, give them the marketing collateral, and all the information, and point out the features—you might even make a sale. But what if you showed up to that same customer to let them know what you're selling will save them money daily, or that it will cut down the time spent on their administrative activities significantly?

It's easier to describe the functionality than it is to really understand what problem they need solving. But connecting with the problem is connecting with the customer.

Just as I know my product inside out, you know your product really well. I could talk for hours about different coaching techniques and coaches that I've worked with. It was the same when I worked in mortgage—my coworkers and I could talk ad nauseam about the mortgage process. But doing so is missing the point.

You're not falling in love with the problem; you feel that the value is in your solution, completely disregarding the possibility that the value for your potential customer is in being heard, having their problem acknowledged, and building trust.

Enough About The Widgets!

My guess is, if you're buying into the "content marketing" myth, you're wasting a lot of time. Thinking you need to educate on process and solution only moves you further and further away from your client's problem.

You also blend in with all the other people who are saying the same thing. You will not be the only business

"I'M TOLD THAT THE MORE VALUE I DELIVER PRE-SALE..."

saying, "Look at all the widgets on my fancy product!" You're competing on something that's copiable. You might have a widget that your competition doesn't have, but give them a minute and they'll have it too. When you're selling on features, you're selling on something that is not differentiated and is easily replicated.

Educating on features or processes is something anybody can do. By taking this approach, you are putting yourself square in the sea-of-many.

Speaking from experience, it's very frustrating. When I struggle to communicate my value, I feel frustrated. You know you're really good at what you do, so why are you having such a hard time convincing people?

The effort of having to convince people is like begging for a second date. You feel like you're always under pressure to dance better. This prevents real connection with your ideal client, for whom you know you perform well.

Many times, this is where price pressure comes from. The problem becomes apparent when you're feature selling. If all features are equal, the differentiator is price.

If I've educated you on all the wonderful things about my widget and the person next to me did the same thing, but theirs is cheaper, you're probably going with cheaper.

Case Study: Give Them The Healthy Big Mac

Remember Marie, my diet clinician client from Chapter 2? She had been trying to reach her ideal clients through content, and it was getting her nowhere. She shared information on what would happen if people didn't seek out the healthy changes she was ready to help them with. She shared loads of content about her process, about the solutions she offered, and the amazing medical benefits, only to get limited views and even less engagement.

She needed to communicate in a way that resonated with the right client, while eliminating people wanting crash diets or to just take a pill and not make the lifestyle changes. Those people are not her clients.

She decided to take a new approach. Instead of sharing another news article featuring the latest rates of diabetes, she made a popular brunch recipe on video. She posted it to social media and got 1000 views. She then made a healthy version of a Big Mac and got another 1000 views. Her potential customers feared diabetes, but they feared having to eat bad diet food and being hungry more.

You can't tell from watching the videos what it will be like when you walk in her clinic or the kinds of restrictions she's about to suggest in her programs. You don't know the eight steps you have to go through before you can eat on your own for life. What she's showing her potential clients now is how she works to solve their biggest perceived diet problems: Constant hunger and terrible food.

Her competitors continue to push out ads telling people how their process works and how much it costs.

"I'M TOLD THAT THE MORE VALUE I DELIVER PRE-SALE..."

When she shifted her messaging from, "Here's all of this scary information," to "Here's your problem that I can solve," everything started to change. Transformation, not information, differentiated her in a pretty busy space.

It's easy to think we have to educate on our spectacular solutions and we'll be guaranteed a sale, but it's simply not the case. By thinking this way, you disregard the things that really help you get sales: demonstrating that you understand your client's problem and building their trust in you to be the one to solve it.

Key Takeaways

- Learn to love your client's problem, not your solution.

- Trust is created by listening to and acknowledging people's problems.

- People are looking for transformation, not information.

- Solution offers are for post-sale.

FIND YOUR GENIUS ZONE & DIFFERENTIATE YOUR BUSINESS!

"If you are giving your all to someone and it's not enough, you're giving it to the wrong person"

- **Unknown**

CHAPTER 7

"My Business Needs To Be Everywhere In Order To Get Noticed"

Let me guess...You're on LinkedIn, YouTube, Instagram, Twitter. You have a Facebook page, a Facebook group, and run Facebook ads. Oh, and don't forget about the Google ads.

Everywhere you turn, someone is saying you should be on... [fill in the blank for latest social media platform]. Some folks seem to have it down pat, they put out content at the speed of Gary Vee. You hear them testify that 30% of their clients come from Facebook or Pinterest.

According to the adverts, you should be able to make millions in just five minutes a day with a proven system that took thousands of business owners from zero to hero in just 10 days. "LinkedIn success with one email!" "How to score 1000 followers a day on Facebook with only organic posts!" With all of these claims, how can you not be everywhere on social?

And you think, "I should be able to do that. Am I missing out on client opportunities by not being everywhere?"

But is it really working? By this I mean are you reaching your high-value lifetime clients? Are you bringing in strong leads from all of the time you are putting in? Or does social media have you attempting to crank out content like some kind of organ-grinder monkey?

I can understand if you're stuck in this myth. You've probably been told over and over again that you must be on Facebook, Twitter, Pinterest, LinkedIn—and not just on one or two from this list, but all of them—or you're missing out. I've even heard coaches and business gurus tell people if they're not marketing across all of social media, they're stupid.

Stupid? I know you're not stupid. I also know you don't need the extra stress.

While you want the exposure and the opportunity to be seen, everywhere can lead to nowhere.

Get Out Of Overwhelm!

Trying to market across all of social media will leave you feeling overwhelmed. The very nature of social media is exhausting. You try to keep up with your campaigns, feeling like you should be posting. You post and post, but your content is just scrolled over, vanishing in the never-ending stream of what your audience sees daily.

You wonder if you are hurting your brand. You push out tons of generic content, spray and pray! All it takes is one boring post and you are social media toast. Your ideal client

"MY BUSINESS NEEDS TO BE EVERYWHERE IN ORDER TO GET NOTICED"

has already started to scroll past you. You end up spending a lot of time and never actually reach your customer.

By spreading yourself too broadly across platforms, no one can see or understand clearly what you do. I even know business owners who stopped digital marketing altogether, because they never reached their actual customer.

It can happen in any area of digital marketing. Any non-targeted and general online communication is simply ineffective.

A lady in my networking group asked me for help with her marketing email open rate. She's wonderful. Her business is great, but she emails a poorly thought-out, autoresponder newsletter. It's general, impersonal and incredibly inauthentic to read. It's not achieving the desired results of bringing her potential clients closer to her.

But she is afraid to be open and to show her own experiences. What about "something is better than nothing"? It used to be that any content was good content, just get your name out there. Now people want to see the real you. Authenticity trumps everything.

It's also possible that email marketing was not going to work in her case.

I know that sounds like sacrilege if you've been told you must have an email campaign. But do you? Are your high-value lifetime clients reading their emails? Like advertising to your grandparents on Tik Tok and emailing your 16-year-old niece, the message will be lost if it's on the wrong platform.

When you have been told again and again that you "must" be everywhere, you feel like you should do it. But if you don't really have the time to develop quality content, or it's not in your strengths to be so social, it could actually hurt your business and cause your visibility to shrink.

Go Where Your Customers Are

"Am I messing up?" my realtor client, Rose, wants to know. She's reluctant to monetize her social media. She posts on social, but nothing targeted or consistent about real estate.

We decide to do a project of 10 videos and push it out via Facebook audiences. It worked great, and now she has an evergreen set of videos that we have published to a landing page.

A few months later I asked her if she was ready to do another set of videos. "Nope," she said, "You have taught me not to do things I am not good at or don't like doing. I hate doing the videos. My sales numbers are excellent right now, so is it okay if we don't? Can I just have another client appreciation dinner instead?"

I asked her if she felt she was meeting her clients where they are and also in her strengths. "Yes!" she replied. So of

"MY BUSINESS NEEDS TO BE EVERYWHERE IN ORDER TO GET NOTICED"

course, I say yes too. For some people social media is just a cake topper.

"My husband says I post too much on Facebook." Enter realtor number two, Betty. She is on Facebook three or four times a day. Client stories, grandkid stories, my husband-thinks-I-talk-too-much stories. She loves it. Her clients love it. Thirty percent of her clients come from these posts. Is she on Insta or Pinterest? Nope. Any ads or remarketing? Nope. Betty shows up as herself, doing something she likes to do, where her clients are and it works really well.

Let's talk about realtor number three, Sophia, who hates all social media. I cannot convince her to post anything. I think her last Facebook or Instagram was five years ago. How's her business? You probably guessed, she does very well. Phone calls, note cards and client parties are how she keeps up with her data base. And that's where they are, not on social.

If you're on all social media platforms, running ads, jumping on people's podcasts, and on top of it all, doing some other offline marketing, but you're still not reaching your customer, why is this?

It is because you are not understanding and thereby targeting your customer. When you don't understand your customer, you cannot speak directly to their needs. Think of it this way, if you were a brick and mortar store, where would you set up? Where would you get the most bang for your buck? Wouldn't it be worth applying that same level of strategy to your digital marketing?

Don't let fear of missing out lead you further into this myth. The message is going to come at you in every direction, "You better be on Facebook. You better be emailing. You better get your message out or you're missing out." But what are you missing out on? Are you just replacing cold calling hundreds of people with cold posting to thousands?

You might worry that by avoiding digital marketing altogether you're going to appear out of touch or, worse, stupid. You don't want to be embarrassed for not keeping up with the times. But what good is blasting yourself across all of the Internet if you have no strategy behind it?

Missed Opportunity Is Always Missed

Setting yourself up so you are marketing across all the platforms is a good way to waste time and money. You risk wearing your audience out with boring content. Before you know it, you have more "unsubscribes" than "likes."

Be careful of sacrificing more effective old-school marketing approaches because you believe digital marketing is the only method, whether it works with your strengths or not. By not working to your strengths and developing a marketing campaign that effectively blends analog and digital marketing tactics, you're missing out on opportunities and limiting yourself.

"MY BUSINESS NEEDS TO BE EVERYWHERE IN ORDER TO GET NOTICED"

Throwing yourself all over the internet also indicates a lack of strategy. What would it look like to 80/20 your marketing? What are your strengths? Are you better live, written, or visual? How are you in "real life"? If you can translate that onto the platform where your ideal client lives, you're going to have the greatest impact.

By putting yourself everywhere, you're completely disregarding your own strengths, authenticity, and unique voice. Now your message gets muddled and you are selling to everyone. You can end up paying a lot of money for subpar leads.

You're quite likely a consumer just as much as a creator when it comes to social media, so consider: Who do you follow that you will watch anytime, anywhere? What's something you like or want? As an example, I might see a boring ad pop up after I visited a website the day before, and because I wasn't really the target audience, I'll just choose to have Facebook remove the ad. But when I see something I really wanted but forgot about pop up in my Facebook again today, I'm not asking Facebook to remove the ad, I'm clicking through!

FIND YOUR GENIUS ZONE & DIFFERENTIATE YOUR BUSINESS!

Case Study: More Leads In Half The Time

My friend Jim is a home remodeler with whom I've had several great conversations about marketing. His company has a Google pay-per-click ad system; they also advertise on Facebook and through an industry app called Houzz.

Last year, Jim worked with an agency and spent $30,000 on SEO and pay-per-click ads. The agency broadcast Jim's company across several platforms, but it wasn't translating into more leads. The results weren't showing up for the amount of money he was investing. Shouldn't the increase in platforms increase the leads?

This year, Jim decided to hire an in-house marketer. Stacey began in January, and by June she had gotten more leads than the agency had the entire year prior. In half the time, Stacey doubled the results of the expensive agency.

How did she do it? For starters, she changed the company newsletter to be more personal. The old newsletter only talked about the business. Now, they shared what Jim and the company were doing in the community. The content on their website was updated—they offered a great lead magnet for potential customers to download. Social media content was targeted, which meant the right customers became engaged, and Jim's SEO finally kicked in. As a result, they got more leads of better quality.

By making the newsletter personal and more authentic, and sending it to the right people, along with updating their website and social media content, Jim got more leads in six months than he did in the entire year of working with the $30,000 agency and the pay-per-click strategy.

"MY BUSINESS NEEDS TO BE EVERYWHERE IN ORDER TO GET NOTICED"

Jim's story reiterates what sets good marketing apart: It connects us with the right customer in an authentic and personal way. When you send your message out all across the world wide web, without aiming it at a direct audience, you reach "anyone," not your ideal client. Marketing everywhere is not unlike playing the numbers game. Ultimately, putting your business everywhere just gets your business nowhere.

Key Takeaways

- Broadcasting a clear and authentic message across a few key platforms is better than trying to market everywhere.

- Find out where your customers spend their time online and deliver your message in those places.

- Apply the 80/20 principle and figure out which 20% of your activities bring the best results.

    "Efficiency is doing things right; effectiveness is doing the right things."

    - Peter Drucker

CHAPTER 8

"I Need To Be Price Competitive To Win The Sale"

In the year 2006 AD, I made a pilgrimage to the Gucci Flagship store in NYC, the mothership of handbag stores. Having finished my best month ever in sales, as a gift to myself I wanted a black Gucci handbag with a bamboo handle.

The bag checked all of my boxes, from the exquisite construction to the status symbol associated with the bamboo handle—and the ability to treat myself to it. I had wanted that bag for over a year. I promised myself I would buy it when I hit my big three goals: zero debt, highest sales in the office and filling up my savings.

When it came time to make the purchase, do you think I asked the sales lady what the price was? No. I gleefully handed her my credit card, and she wrapped up my bag.

Walking out of the store, the experience had me thinking, the price of a handbag at Target is always checked. Do I really want to pay $19 for this? At Gucci, there was a line of people just handing over their credit card.

Is your business a Gucci or a Target? If you're competing on price, you can be sure you're a Target.

FIND YOUR GENIUS ZONE & DIFFERENTIATE YOUR BUSINESS!

The Cookie Is Never Enough

Nothing wrong with Target—I love that place. But unless you are a volume seller, competing on price is always the lowest common denominator. There's an old adage, "You give a mouse a cookie, and they come back for milk." Because the cookie is never enough and neither is your lowest price.

In the past, whenever I told potential clients I'd give them a discount on their rate just to close the sale, suddenly they didn't want to pay the lender fee. It was never enough. The more I told myself I had to do whatever it takes to close the deal—because all of something is better than none of nothing—the more I attracted clients because they too wanted the discount rate and they didn't want to pay any fees.

What was I doing wrong to attract these clients? Knowing what I know now, it's obvious to me that I had not communicated the problem I solve for these clients in a clear, trustworthy way.

If you are not effectively communicating the problem you are solving to your market, you are attracting people based on price. From here, it's easy to make the mistake of telling prospects all the things you do in your process to make your price worth it to them. Now you're stuck trying to validate your fee, which always leads to, "Can I get a lower price?" You haven't communicated to them that you solve

"I NEED TO BE PRICE COMPETITIVE TO WIN THE SALE"

their exact problem, nor have you built the trust required for them to know you're the one they want to solve it.

Instead, you are trying to build trust by telling your customers everything you're going to do for them, rather than listening to your customers and communicating how you are the one who can get to the bottom of their problem. (Or, in the case of my Gucci, scratch their itch.)

It is easy to get caught up in price, competing in the same way; it's easy to believe you just have to work harder to get ahead. It seems easier to compete on price than to turn business away because your values are not aligned with that particular customer.

Offering a discount is possibly the easiest thing to do in business. Just cut the price. But it's not like we're selling commodities here. If you're selling pencils, okay, I get it. You sell the cheapest pencil. But we are not talking about being a price simplifier. Have you noticed things that become iconic in the marketplace, like the iPhone, rarely go on sale?

One Size Does Not Fit All

Sometimes when I see business owners struggling with this problem, it's because they haven't thought out their own unique pricing strategy. It's easy to assume that one-size-fits-all when it comes to sales.

Thinking one-size-fits-all ignores the problem your clients are having to begin with. Not everyone can do for your clients what you can; but if you don't speak to the problem, they will never know this. When I worked in mortgage, obviously I needed to help people get a loan. But what problem was I really solving?

After a conversation with a client, I might learn they messed up their credit and now they're scared they won't be approved for the mortgage and they have to be out of their house in two months, and their partner is pretty darn angry with them.

Considering this, I'm not really getting them a mortgage loan. I am solving a keep-you-awake-for-weeks, "How will I ever fix this, I'm such an idiot! No way my wife's not leaving me!" problem. Do you really think they're going to ask me how much that costs? No. But if they do not trust me to solve it, they absolutely will.

Be Like Gucci

When you compete on price or apply discounts to your products and services, you are also putting your market at risk. I came across an article in Forbes magazine on destroying your brand. At that time Coach and Michael Kors, both brands that could have been as esteemed as Gucci over time, decided instead to flood the market with low-priced handbags. Now you can walk into any discount store (we love you TJ Maxx!) and see a 13-year-old buy a

"I NEED TO BE PRICE COMPETITIVE TO WIN THE SALE"

Coach bag for $40 that you just bought for $400 in their corporate store.

Coach and Michael Kors suffered a significant loss financially as well as to their reputations. Shareholders were not amused. Do you think anyone is paying full price for a Coach bag the way I paid full price, with delight, for my Gucci bag? Not so much.

Price competing diminished the perceived quality of those brands, and it could do the same to your brand. It can wear away at your self-confidence and you will continue attracting the wrong customers.

In discounting your prices so much, it's not long before you become a minimum-wage employee. You've worked so hard but given so much discount, you might as well get a job at Trader Joe's. At least they have benefits! Your reputation is at stake, because now you've become a discount broker/ company/ service.

Even worse, what if you have to fire one of those bad customers or clients? A client pulled in at a discount price is guaranteed not to be your ideal client. Now you're trapped with a difficult client and it's impossible to end the relationship. They aren't leaving without that discount!

Once you start playing the price game, it becomes harder and harder to push your rates back up. Your integrity comes into question because clients are used to you playing the game. When you quote your rate and they ask if they can get it lower, you're faced with a decision that will directly impact your integrity and trustworthiness. You told your client you were going to give your best price the first time, and now, at their request, you're giving a discount? This is a surefire way to break down trust.

Case Study: A Tale Of Two Loan Officers

Price competing is really just competing, period. It will always keep you locked in a world where there are winners and losers.

Take my mortgage loan officer colleagues, Mike and Jay. One day, while discussing interest rates, Mike told me he had stopped bringing up rates with his clients altogether. "If they bring up the rate, I messed up," he said. It stopped me in my tracks. We were in a very competitive market. How often was that the first or second question I'd hear from my clients?

But Mike got it. He told me he helps them solve their problem. He focuses on building a trustworthy relationship with the person referring the client to him, so he is already on strong footing when it comes to trust. Once he meets the client, he asks them what they need and what their goals are.

In a typical interaction, Mike starts with "What can I do for you?" and from there, he acknowledges their problems. Then he asks them if they're ready to move forward with him as the trusted solution. Only when they say yes does he send them documents, a couple of which have the rate on them.

Now let's talk about Jay. Jay wanted to emulate Mike, who was closing deals and not competing at all on price. Jay hadn't yet figured out

"I NEED TO BE PRICE COMPETITIVE TO WIN THE SALE"

how to attract his ideal client. He would choose realtors who had a ton of business and could refer to him. No matter who the realtor was or what they valued, if they were closers, Jay was picking them.

He ended up choosing successful realtors, but they were used to being catered to, given gifts and getting whatever they wanted in exchange for their clients. Jay eventually closed one of these realtors, but every time she sent him a deal it came with an order: "Do whatever you can to keep this deal."

Soon it became clear that no matter what Jay did, it was never enough for her. At one point she had the nerve to tell him the gifts he sent her weren't expensive enough.

And that was just the realtor! Meanwhile, the client who's been referred by this realtor assumes they too can get whatever they want. Now Jay is going back and forth on interest rate.

Little did we know, our main competitor's loan officer was going after the same realtors as Jay. Their sales manager had told this loan officer to do whatever it took to get the business. Just beat Jay!

We found out they were taking up to three percentage point losses on their loans in order to beat him and get those deals!

Jay was purely going after business. It wasn't his fault. That's what he was told to do. He was told to find the one closing the most deals and tell her he'll run as hard as she wanted him to run for her clients. There was no loyalty or trust in the relationship. The realtors and their clients continually went straight to price. He was price competing with our company's arch-nemeses, who were willing to beat him, at any cost.

FIND YOUR GENIUS ZONE & DIFFERENTIATE YOUR BUSINESS!

Who can sustain that game?

Contrast Jay with Mike. Mike sought out people who wanted to refer clients to someone they trust. People who were kind and had excellent systems and communication.

Most importantly, Mike never talked about price. He had a different attitude about it. He did not approach his work as a competition. He knew he needed to find people with whom he value-aligned. He sold to potential clients specifically on what he had to offer that was in his strengths and values, things he excelled at delivering. It had nothing to do with price.

Mike also truly believed in what he offered. He worked diligently on his system and his process. His entire approach became his ticket out of the price competition game. Believe me, the price game is not worth playing. What will be your ticket out?

Key Takeaways

- Price competing is competing at the lowest common denominator.

- Develop a pricing strategy based on your needs, as well as the needs of your clients and the market.

- Solving your client's problem and building trust will leave you hearing, "Where do I sign?" more often than, "How much does it cost?".

"I NEED TO BE PRICE COMPETITIVE…"

"The more you focus on the value of your product or service, the less important the price becomes."

–Brian Tracy

CHAPTER 9

"I Have To Play The Sales Game And Use Typical Sales Techniques"

"Roberta, we're friends, right?"

I'm not sure, I thought. How was I supposed to answer that?

"Yeah, sure," I replied hesitantly.

"Great. Then I'm going to need you to do this for me."

"Um, okay…" I answered, feeling choiceless again.

My sales coach was teaching us how to say the exact right phrase to get any prospect to reply in an advantageous manner. I learned that if you do it right, you will move them forward. I also learned to never accept a non-answer. Questions should advance them to a yes.

As my sales coach said repeatedly, wouldn't it be nice if everyone said "yes" all the time?

Would it, I would think to myself, really?

Mr. Sales Coach told us it's not manipulation if it's true. Oddly enough, at the end of the day, I felt manipulated by him. Was he lying about his intentions? If what he was teaching was true, would I have felt so icky or insulted?

At the time, I surmised I had a lot to learn to be able to "move people forward." I needed to get over my "sales

FIND YOUR GENIUS ZONE & DIFFERENTIATE YOUR BUSINESS!

reluctance." "Grow up, Roberta!" I told myself. "Put on your big girl pants and SELL! SELL! SELL!"

I have since learned, as it turns out, people like to move themselves forward. They often regret the purchases and agreements they feel maneuvered into.

So why do we still think this is how to make a sale?

Rewrite The ABCs

If you believe you have to play the sales game and use traditional sales tricks and manipulate the customer, chances are you have only been focused on the outcome. It's dehumanizing, both for the customer and you.

"They can sell sand at the beach!" You may have watched the top producer in your field sell what seemed like sand at the beach. As dehumanizing as some sales tactics can be, we see that for some folks, it works.

But selling this way rarely feels right. You're turning your customers into numbers that you have to keep massaging and moving along your sales funnel. No matter how much you know they need your product or service and tell them such, you're still taking away their true choice, their real ability to say, "I want that because I know exactly what it is and I trust you." This can't happen when you're only focused on the outcome.

Old sales techniques are rife with manipulative language and ideas like, "Always keep moving people forward," and,

"I HAVE TO PLAY THE SALES GAME AND USE TYPICAL SALES TECHNIQUES"

"Never take no for an answer." This "always be closing" mentality is really competition and a zero-sum game. You either win or you lose. But we're talking about people here!

If you're only trying to move your prospects along your funnel, you will reach a point where trust has completely broken down. You may find yourself chasing, wondering why no one answers your "just following up" emails. If only you could sell sand at the beach . . .

Of course, it's easy to buy into the idea of, "Wouldn't it be nice if everybody said yes all the time?" But believing this puts you back in the sea-of-many, selling to everyone and playing the numbers game. It also results in dishonest responses, when what you really want is for people to be honest with you. To say yes only when they trust you to solve their problem.

Is there anything worse than a yes or a maybe, when what your prospect wanted to say was NO?

By the time I left Mr. Sales Coach, I actually did feel manipulated. I know he's a good guy, but it left me wondering what his real intentions were. I left never wanting to put someone in a position to feel that way about me.

How many times have you bought a service or product under pressure, and then realized it wasn't the right fit? We always regret the purchases and agreements we feel maneuvered into.

Sell On Trust

Old sales tips like, "Always be closing," "Get five yeses," and "Move them along" can work to a degree, but they won't guarantee the outcome you desire, especially if you want to attract your high-value lifetime clients. They are also ineffective for anyone working within a trust-based selling process. It's not a lack of talent on your part, it's a lack of earned trust from the client.

Don't sell yourself short. If you have something people need, something that is good for them, you want to communicate to them about their problem and do so in a way that reveals if you are aligned in your respective values. This gives customers the choice because, ultimately, it is their choice whether to buy from you or not.

When you don't give your customers a choice, trust will break down every time. I know, it's scary. If you give me a choice, I can say no to you. And you don't want that, you only want the yes. But again, if it's not a fully honest yes, you'll never develop the kinds of clients and the kind of reputation that produces more and more people who trust you, say yes honestly, and refer their friends to you. The definitive win-win scenario.

It takes courage to value what your customers really want and to learn what your customers really need, while also maintaining integrity in the transaction. Doing it well

"I HAVE TO PLAY THE SALES GAME AND USE TYPICAL SALES TECHNIQUES"

means you have to let go of the outcome. You have to focus on their problem over your solution.

Attaching to the outcome is a byproduct of using these old-school sales techniques. They keep you firmly rooted in your ego. You risk getting caught up in all of it, only thinking of what you will get in the end, making it a game. Not letting people be honest with you.

You think you're doing the right thing, but what you're doing mires you in your ego instead of expanding into your heart, which might remind you that you should let your customers decide for themselves.

Still, it seems easier to push customers to the yes, and then worry about everything else afterwards. The fallacy being a complete disregard for the grand mess created when you are not a fit. This mess might include a loss of your reputation and loss of repeat business, wearing out your staff and reducing profits.

That coach I mentioned earlier? I still feel manipulated by him. His reputation is not positive in my eyes, and as a consumer, I could tell others about him and cost him business. I didn't, of course, and I won't—but I could. What kinds of things might people write in their Google reviews if you're maneuvering them to something they didn't fully choose?

You're a customer as much as a business owner. When, as a business owner, you find yourself avoiding the route that leads you to the win-win, consider: How would it feel if someone did it to you? Do you want to feel manipulated or pushed into a yes?

Ultimately, adhering to sales techniques like those demonstrate that you value the outcome more than the person. More and more people can sniff out that kind of salesmanship. Today's consumer does not want to feel manipulated. They definitely don't want to be sold.

There Is No Second Loser

I know business owners who really do see these sales techniques for what they are, and hate using them. They feel trapped. They've bought into the winner/ loser way of thinking and now they're just trying to avoid being first loser. But they hate it because it's completely out of line with their values.

My accountability partner, Daniella, who I mentioned in Chapter 2, is wrestling with this issue right now. She is worried that her sales technique is off, but in reality the scripts she was told to use just aren't working for her. Of course, what's really not working is that these scripts seek to constantly push people forward, and in Daniella's line of work, financial planning, she's talking about their money. They have to trust her. She values the relationship with her clients more than just making the sale.

Does this approach work? Somewhat, although way less than one would have thought. When she persisted with

"I HAVE TO PLAY THE SALES GAME AND USE TYPICAL SALES TECHNIQUES"

using the "proven system" scripts, more and more she found herself feeling as though she were fighting with clients on the phone, trying to convince them to let her solve their problem. It reached the point where she stopped making calls. And this is where her money is coming from!

Maybe Daniella could have sustained it if she didn't value people. But she does. It's the business owners who value money over people that can sustain this kind of sales approach; but even then, it's highly likely they will endure a serious churn of clients and referral partners.

What Daniella is trying to do, build relationships, takes longer. When you want sales and results fast, just like those fad diets we talked about in Chapter 4, churn and burn will get you there faster. But it's most likely unhealthy and ultimately not sustainable.

The financial impact can be high; one reason being customer attrition. Daniella experienced plenty of chargebacks when she worked from the scripts because people were only saying yes to get her off the phone.

Depending on your business model, you might have higher attrition rates than others. But beyond this immediate financial impact, you are also losing out on referrals. Instead of attracting clients who might become your raving fans and referral partners, you end up attracting clients that like manipulation or just want you to stop bothering them.

Referral conversations sound like this: "How is your financial planner? Would you recommend them?"

FIND YOUR GENIUS ZONE & DIFFERENTIATE YOUR BUSINESS!

"Oh, okay . . . I guess we did the right thing. Seems like anyone could have done the work."

Or, just maybe, they could sound like this:

"OMG, we LOVE her! Let me text you her info. You cannot use anyone else."

Which would you rather hear?

Case Study: Jordan Belfort: King Of The Sales Game

Possibly the most damaging aspect of the old-school sales mentality is the competitive attitude where if you're not a winner, you're a loser. It's a win or a loss. Second place is just first loser.

Why do we still buy in? It's been romanticized a bit; the hard-hitting sales legend takes over the city, gets the girl.

But what does this do to a businessperson? In the case of Jordan Belfort, it can become the foundation of your downfall.

I'm sure you've heard of Belfort, now a motivational speaker, who was glamourized in the 2013 Oscar-winning movie *The Wolf of Wall Street*. And while it seems preposterous as a story, the influence lives on. Not too long ago, I had an office down the hall from a young man who had a big picture of Belfort hung in his office for motivation.

Did Belfort's drive and sales approach bring him financial success? Absolutely. Huge parties on yachts filled with bikini-clad women? Check. Making almost $1 million a week at the peak of his career? Check. Ferrari, mansion, envy of all? Check.

"I HAVE TO PLAY THE SALES GAME AND USE TYPICAL SALES TECHNIQUES"

Where did the behaviors and the pressure lead him? Drug addiction and eventual jail time. He managed to turn his life around post-jail; but before he went to jail, his values were very much on money and accumulating it at all costs. There is no doubt in my mind he dehumanized more than a few clients on his way to millions and, really, dehumanized himself. His drive to keep winning, winning, winning led him down the road of addiction and crime.

When I first started in sales, I admired the big dogs. They could sell to anyone. And if not, they didn't mind cursing the naysayers on their way out the door. They drove big European cars, golfed the best courses, and partied it up at the swankiest places—all while working 80 hours a week. They were sales winners!

I later realized they were numbing themselves from lives they hated. Alcohol, prescription drugs, food, gambling, non-stop work, and prestige. For many, it wasn't sustainable. The money they amassed went to divorces, rehab, or bigger houses and more expensive cars to make them feel better.

Look, if you want to charge ahead with old-school sales techniques, vying to be a clear winner, go for it. But you might be reading the wrong book. When you start degrading your morals and disrespecting other people just to be that winner, your integrity gets worn down. It chips away at your reputation. Trust is replaced with suspicion. You lose your self-respect. Your personal integrity. Is any of that worth losing, for the sake of getting someone to say yes?

Key Takeaways

- Games lead to dehumanizing our prospective customers and essentially ourselves.

- Make "win-win" the goal. The sale should produce a win for all involved.

- Instead of focusing on the outcome, focus on your customer's problem and if you are a fit to solve it.

    "Establishing trust is better than any sales technique."

    - Mike Puglia

CHAPTER 10

"I Can Solve My Own Business Challenges. I Don't Need Any Help"

After the 2008 housing crash, those of us in the mortgage industry found ourselves reinventing our businesses. The housing landscape had shifted so much, and the mortgage market itself was changing every day. Many of us, myself included, struggled to keep up with the fallout of the housing crisis as it ripped through the industry.

I definitely needed help. Still, when my boss approached me asking if I wanted help, I said no. I knew I needed it, but I also knew I didn't want more education on the old business model, which is what he would have offered. It wasn't just help I needed, but a whole new way of approaching my work.

One sunny day an invitation arrived in my inbox. An invitation to learn a new way of getting clients. I RSVPed right away—Yes! A few weeks later I found myself at the end of their three-day seminar faced with an offer once again. Only this time, the offer spoke directly to me. It was as if they knew my exact problem. They offered solutions

I hadn't dreamed of, and a level of support I had no idea I needed until I felt it in that seminar.

I was so happy when I wrote the check that I was teary-eyed. That group revealed to me that possibly even more than a new approach, what I really needed was support.

After all, much like you, I'm not dumb, I can read a manual. I can find information. I can follow someone who is further ahead on the path, observe what worked for them and apply the same technique. But the accountability? The validation? The community? The consistent support? All of these were what I really needed.

Essentially, I was writing that check for somebody to hold my hand while I grew my new business. I already had a solid foundation and knew the principles I wanted to incorporate. What I needed most was someone to help me dig down deeper. That's precisely what that coaching group gave me. To this day, the investment was one of the best things I have ever done for myself.

Get Out Of Isolation

As a business owner, when you're out there busting your buns day after day trying to keep the ship afloat, it can feel incredibly isolating. By not getting help and support when you need it, it seems impossible to reach the next level.

You know you need more sales or to hire somebody to take over the administrative work, but you're continually

"I CAN SOLVE MY OWN BUSINESS CHALLENGES. I DON'T NEED ANY HELP"

pushing up against barriers. Try though you might, you just can't seem to get past them. It's discouraging. You're smart, you can figure it out, but for some reason your business is just not moving forward in a meaningful way.

Maybe you are spending too much time working in the business or on activities outside of your $1000/ hour work. We all know that working on our $1000/ hour (or $10,000/ hour) work should be priority number one, well ahead of the $10/hour stuff. But it is much easier said than done.

Sure, we all have to work in the business somewhat when first starting out. But at some point, you have to get out of the trenches. More often than not, business owners seeking coaching are not trying to get help to move from A to B, rather they want help moving from B to C and C to D.

Running a business can feel like a solitary journey. You don't know what you don't know until you know it, after all. You forget just how impactful it can be to have somebody there with you, somebody who has walked the road you are on, somebody to help you when you can't see the forest for the trees. Someone to take the blinders off and help us see outside of what we have been working so diligently on.

In my life, just having someone to say, "Hey, have you thought about this?" proved invaluable.

Still Fighting For It

All of the world's top performers have coaches, from Anthony Robbins to Tom Brady to Barack Obama. Oprah, who has countless mentors, often references Maya Angelou as her life coach. Beyond just the world of athletics, any top performer in any industry has a coach behind them, guaranteed.

Some coaching feels like rearranging deck chairs. You have heard what they are saying over and over, but is it just another shiny object available for purchase?

What most business owners need is to get down to the bottom of things, figure out why what was working at one time just isn't working any longer.

One Last Grand Slam

Tennis champion Serena Williams found herself sitting in the locker room when she should have been out on the court. A resounding defeat to someone ranked 100 places lower than her in the first round of the French Open had left her reeling.

Multiple injuries and losses dragged on for the once highly motivated champion. But as we all know, Serena was not meant for losing. At this point, she had 13 Grand Slam titles under her belt. What the HELL was going on!

"I CAN SOLVE MY OWN BUSINESS CHALLENGES. I DON'T NEED ANY HELP"

Not one to feel sorry for herself, she did what most high-level athletes would do—she hired a coach. Even with the issues that had plagued her over the last few years, she was ready to rejuvenate her career. Serena was not even close to finished yet.

New coach Patrick Mouratoglou took a direct approach with the champion tennis player. He laid down the rules on the first day. Knowing Serena's no BS approach to life, he refused to let the tennis star set the tone.

Recounting their first session, he says she was tough, but he required that she open up and fully participate. She did and won Wimbledon that year, along with Olympic gold and the US Open. Since then she has battled her way to within one win from a record-breaking 24th Grand Slam.

Patrick's motto is posted prominently on his website: "We are accountable for our players' achievements, and it is up to us to take responsibility for them, both in victory and defeat."

What's interesting here, is Serena has stalled again. It's hard to stay motivated and keep up with the younger players on the court. Mouratoglou answered reporters that Serena still has it in her, and they both know it. But they also know what they are doing isn't producing the same results as before. So it's time so switch it up again. Change some tactics to match who she is right now in her game, not her game five years ago.

FIND YOUR GENIUS ZONE & DIFFERENTIATE YOUR BUSINESS!

Mouratoglou credits shared values for much of their partnership success. Loyalty, accountability and trust keep them working together even when it's time to change strategies . . . again.

A good coach will help you get ahead. Take a few strokes off of your swing, they used to say. A great coach takes you as you are, with the strengths you have right now, and helps you win again, but differently.

Like Serena, it may be your second or third time around, but you are older now, more experienced. You don't put up with what you used to, and you just can't muscle through it any longer either.

But who wants to brute force it anymore? That "work hard and it will be okay" game is for those who don't have enough maturity to know that it will not solve all ills. What does is applying principles like 80/20 to solve problems. Working in accountability and trust. Then taking the time for rest and play. Rejuvenation.

For a business owner, the worst-case scenario if you don't get this kind of help is waking up one morning, 10 years from now, and recognizing that your business hasn't changed or grown in any meaningful way since the last day you felt like you were winning.

Do you really want to be wrestling the same alligator 10 years from now?

"I CAN SOLVE MY OWN BUSINESS CHALLENGES. I DON'T NEED ANY HELP"

Investing In Yourself Yields The Best Returns

Like most business owners, you probably value your independence. You should be able to figure it out yourself, right? You can read the book. You can watch the webinars.

Why do you need somebody to push you along?

We may know what to do, or at least know where to find out how, but knowledge is usually not the problem.

"Roberta, if you were opening a bakery, no one would blame you for buying an oven, even an expensive one." Coach Peg B. handed me one of the best pieces of advice I received on starting my coaching business. It's scary to think about putting money out to invest in ourselves. But the best rate of return always comes from investing in ourselves.

Some of us were brought up to invest in ourselves last. To just work harder and it will all work out. Or if we were good enough, we would not need help. I know I was brought up in these myths. They kept me exhausted and behind the eight ball for years!

As the Zen proverb goes, "When the student is ready, the teacher will appear." For me, that teacher was a coach.

FIND YOUR GENIUS ZONE & DIFFERENTIATE YOUR BUSINESS!

Case Study: My Story

Not getting help or working with the right coach could leave you missing out on achieving your full potential. I know this was true for me.

When my manager asked me if I needed help and I told him no, I still knew I needed help. I regretted saying it. He was being kind, and he genuinely wanted to help me, and I knew I needed it, although I also knew he would have just given me the old school sales techniques. So while I knew I needed help, it wasn't the right kind of help.

When I saw the ad for the coaching group that I eventually went with, I knew I'd found the right group for me. I went to the workshop and then read the entire book. I consumed all of the information. And while I could have done everything myself, there I was, signing that check for support, and feeling great about it.

While I valued the information, more importantly I valued finding a community of like-minded people who knew how I felt. I wasn't about to leave. A colleague pointed out to me that I wasn't looking for information, I was looking for transformation.

He was completely right. What I had been doing in my business was not working. I needed so much more than just another book telling me how to run a business.

Before joining the coaching group, I was miserable in my job. But I was the only one paying my bills. There was no calling my parents for money. I had to make it work. So, I persevered and made it through 10 years of crazy in the mortgage business, coming out the other side. But I couldn't keep fighting the battle by myself anymore or sustain the way I had been struggling.

"I CAN SOLVE MY OWN BUSINESS CHALLENGES. I DON'T NEED ANY HELP"

The first thing the coaches did was tell me to stop doing pretty much everything I had been doing. They showed me a massive change in mindset, and it took a while for me to fully integrate this new way of thinking. Like most meaningful change, it did not come overnight.

But change did come over time. I came face to face with the truth that mortgage was just not for me. I had built my business for the third time, then moved to another state, and I built it again. The day came when my coach said to me, "Roberta why are you doing something you really don't want to do anymore?" After 20 years in mortgage, it was time to move on.

The skills I learned from coaching profoundly changed my approach to business. I learned to 80/20 my processes. I got clear on my values. I learned how to tell when a potential client was not aligned with my values and the relationship wouldn't work, which saved me endless hours catering to clients that would have been a mismatch for all involved.

The greatest gifts I received from being coached, however, include self-awareness, and reaching a place of 100% honesty with myself. This allowed me to make serious money and enjoy my life NOW.

As I said earlier, I don't believe passion or hard work are the "cure all," as we are told so often. But I do believe that values alignment, working in our gifts and strengths, and improving what's best in ourselves will steer us toward our meaningful work. This is the work that makes us whatever amount of money we desire, work we can do in balance with enjoying life and enjoying it right now, not when the difficulties of business building are over, so many years from now.

It's not a promise of perfection; all lives have their trials and tribulations. The goal is to be in a healthy place, personally and professionally, when the trials come. This is what will sustain you. Whereas living a life that everyone on the outside thinks is enviable, while on the inside you are miserable, or worse, numb, will not provide the core strength that you need.

Stronger Together

Coaching took me to a place where I could see what I wanted to do and whom I wanted to become based on my values, my strengths and my most authentic self. I let go of what others define as "winning" and "losing," which allows me to default to finding the win-win in any sales situation.

Coaching also led me to the sweet spot, where I was able to make the living I wanted. Whether that's $60,000 a year or $60 million a year, coaching is what gets me there—and I can do it all by working in my values and my strengths.

I know you can reach the place where you, too, can earn the living you want, live the life you want, and work in your values and strengths, your unique genius zone. It's difficult to reach this place alone. Support, accountability, community, education, and, most of all, that second set of

"I CAN SOLVE MY OWN BUSINESS CHALLENGES. I DON'T NEED ANY HELP"

eyes, that second perspective a coach offers, are all essential pieces to achieving success in business.

The goal is harmony in life. It's not about building a work-life balance, where your work is on one end of the seesaw and your life on the other. Investing in yourself through working with a coach is the path to reaching your full potential and expanding your life and business in ways you may not even imagine right now.

Success on your own terms and the harmonious life you seek are waiting for you. The question is: are you ready to find your genius zone?

Key Takeaways

- Excellence is rarely achieved alone. As the African proverb goes, "If you want to go fast, go alone. If you want to go far, go together."

- Investing in yourself is the best way to find and work from your genius zone.

- Coaching can help you find your meaningful work and help you find harmony to enjoy your life now.

> "If we are actively phenomenologically [using direct experience] creating our own reality, why wouldn't you make it the one you like?"
>
> **- Dr. Tom Sweeney**

If this book has resonated with you and you are ready to shift your thinking and differentiate your business to become a category-of-one, then visit www.RobertaRavella.com/Consult for your Complimentary Business Growth Strategy Consultation (value $795.00).

NOTES

NOTES

NOTES

NOTES

www.ingramcontent.com/pod-product-compliance
Lightning Source LLC
Chambersburg PA
CBHW070649220526
45466CB00001B/366